CERTIFICATE IN BOOKKEEPING AND ACCOUNTS

(COMPUTERISED)

Institute of Certified Bookkeepers

Level III

British Library Cataloguing-in-Publication Data

A catalogue record for this book is available from the British Library.

Published by:

Kaplan Publishing UK
Unit 2 The Business Centre
Molly Millars Lane
Wokingham
RG41 2QZ

ISBN 978-1-78415-192-8

© Kaplan Financial Limited, 2014

Printed and bound in Great Britain.

CONTENTS

INTRODUCTION

STUDY TEXT

This study text has been specially prepared for the Institute of Certified Bookkeepers Computerised Bookkeeping and Accounts Level III qualification.

It uses a case study approach to guide you through the syllabus and builds up your knowledge and skills chapter by chapter. The text is based upon Sage Instant Account V19, but can also be followed if you are using Sage Line 50 or other versions of Sage Instant Accounts.

Quality and accuracy are of the utmost importance to us so if you spot an error in any of our products, please send an email to mykaplanreporting@kaplan.com with full details, or follow the link to the feedback form in MyKaplan.

Our Quality Co-ordinator will work with our technical team to verify the error and take action to ensure it is corrected in future editions.

SYLLABUS

Syllabus

The Level III Certificate in Bookkeeping and Accounts covers the preparation of ledger balances, control accounts and reconciliations, adjustments and preparation of final accounts for non-incorporated businesses or organisations.

The ICB has stated that the Level III Certificate in Bookkeeping and Accounts unit is designed to equip students with the knowledge and skills they need for the role of an employed or self-employed bookkeeper, be able to reconcile bank statements with the ledgers, produce a VAT return, control the sales and purchases ledgers, post year-end adjustments and produce the final accounts for a sole trader, partnership and not-for-profit organisation in both a manual and a computerised system.

This study text covers all the aspects of computerised bookkeeping included in the syllabus.

Manual Bookkeeping and Accounts for Level III is covered in a separate study text.

Learning objectives

On completion of the Level III Certificate in Bookkeeping and Accounts, the student will be able to:

- Understand the following areas of underpinning knowledge:
    - The importance of adhering to a set of ethical principles
    - How and when to take action to cope with unethical behaviour
    - The concepts of business entity, going concern, historical cost, consistency, prudence and accruals
    - The legal requirements for forming a partnership
    - Different ways of processing VAT for EU and non-EU transactions
    - Alternative VAT systems e.g. VAT margin scheme

- Prepare a bank reconciliation statement

- Understand the purpose and use of control accounts as a checking mechanism

- Account for VAT and prepare a VAT return

- Prepare a ledger account to record the disposal of a fixed asset and to calculate the profit or loss on disposal

- Calculate adjustments to the accounts including:

  - Opening and closing stock

  - Depreciation of fixed assets

  - Accruals and pre-payments

  - Provision for doubtful debts

- Prepare the final accounts for a non-incorporated business including processing of adjustments for opening and closing stock, depreciation, accruals, prepayments, provision for doubtful debts in the following areas:

  - Sole trader

  - Partnership

  - Not-for-Profit Organisation

Learning Outcomes and Assessment criteria

The unit consists of five Learning Outcomes which are further broken down into Assessment criteria.

The manual elements of these learning outcomes are covered in a separate study text.

The Learning Outcomes for both the manual and the computerised elements of Level III, as well as their assessment criteria, are listed below:

Topic 1 – Underpinning knowledge	
Learning Outcome	**Assessment Criteria**

1.1 Understand the importance of adhering to a code of ethical principles	Be able to:
	
	• understand the importance of adhering to a set of professional ethics when working with clients, suppliers, colleagues and others with regards to:
	
	    – integrity and honesty
	    – objectivity
	    – professional competence and due care and diligence
	    – confidentiality
	    – professional behaviour including separating personal duties from business life
	    – adhering to organisational codes of practice and regulations
	    – working within own professional experience, knowledge and expertise

1.2 Understand when and how to take appropriate action to cope with unethical behaviour	Be able to: • identify relevant authorities to whom unethical behaviour, suspected illegal acts or other malpractice should be reported • identify inappropriate client behaviour and how to report it to relevant authorities • explain the procedure which should be followed if it is suspected that an act has been committed which is believed to be unethical, or illegal
1.3 Understand the legal differences between the structures of various types of businesses	Be able to: • understand the nature of liability for sole traders and partners • define the term partnership • identify the characteristics of a partnership agreement • understand the rules that apply in the absence of a partnership agreement • identify the characteristics of not-for-profit organisations and their accounting requirements

1.4 Understand the main accounting concepts that apply	Be able to: • identify and explain the concepts of: – business entity, going concern, historical cost, consistency, prudence, accruals • identify the method of producing accounts for those businesses who may declare income under the simpler income tax regime for the simplest small businesses
1.5 Understand the different rules that apply when processing VAT transactions	Be able to: • understand that there are different schemes for applying VAT such as: – annual accounting scheme – flat rate scheme – retail scheme – partial exemption – VAT margin scheme Note: questions will not be set testing data entry or completion of VAT returns for such schemes

Topic 2 – Reconciliation of accounts and correction of errors

Learning Outcome	**Assessment Criteria**
2.1 Reconcile supplier statements	Be able to: • reconcile supplier statements with the accounts
2.2 Prepare a bank reconciliation statement	In both a manual and computerised system, be able to: • compare individual items on the bank statement with those in the cash book • up-date the cash book • prepare the bank reconciliation statement
2.3 Use control accounts to reconcile sales and purchase ledgers	In both a manual and computerised system, be able to: • reconcile sales and purchase ledger control accounts with totals from the subsidiary ledgers to check the accuracy of the ledgers

KAPLAN PUBLISHING

2.4 Understand the need to correct errors	Be able to: • understand what to do if the trial balance does not balance • open a suspense account where applicable to account for any imbalance in the trial balance • identify and correct errors, including the correct treatment for VAT, that do not affect the trial balance e.g. omission, commission, principle, original entry, reversal, compensating • prepare and clear the suspense account as appropriate • produce a corrected trial balance • prepare journal entries for the above errors • post relevant corrections in a computerised system

Topic 3 – VAT Returns

Learning Outcome	Assessment Criteria
3.1 Reconcile the VAT account	In both a manual and computerised system, be able to: • reconcile the VAT return figures with the VAT account
3.2 Complete a VAT return	In both a manual and computerised system, be able to: complete and submit a VAT return (standard and/or cash VAT only)

Topic 4 – Calculate and post adjustments to the ledgers

Learning Outcome	Assessment Criteria
4.1 Calculate depreciation	Be able to: • calculate depreciation on a fixed asset using both straight line and reducing balance method • calculate the original cost price of an asset given net book value and depreciation rates and number of years of depreciation

4.2 Account for the disposal of fixed assets	In both a manual and computerised system, be able to: • correctly identify the original cost of the asset disposed of • correctly identify and record all disposal costs and revenues in the appropriate accounts • correctly calculate and determine the cumulative depreciation to date on a disposal • prepare the disposal account • determine profit and or loss on sale of the asset • make relevant journal entries to record the disposal

4.3 Understand the need to allow for adjustments to the accounts	In both a manual and computerised system, be able to:
	• post entries to the ledgers for the following adjustments:
	  – opening and closing stock including valuing stock at the lower of cost and net realisable value
	  – accruals and pre-payments including dealing with the relevant entries in the following year
	  – depreciation (straight line and reducing balance)
	  – account for the revaluation of fixed assets
	  – provision for doubtful debts account including
	    – identifying the need to provide such a provision
	    – calculating the provision
	    – accounting for both an increase and decrease in the provision
	    – preparing the relevant journal entry

Topic 5 – Final accounts of non-incorporated businesses	
Learning Outcome	**Assessment Criteria**
5.1 Prepare a set of final accounts for a sole trader from a given trial balance	In both a manual and computerised system, be able to: • prepare a trading and profit and loss account from a trial balance to include adjustments • prepare a Balance Sheet showing clearly the main categories of assets and liabilities • close down the revenue accounts at the year end
5.2 Prepare a set of final accounts for 'not-for-profit' organisations	In both a manual and computerised system, be able to: • prepare an opening statement of affairs • distinguish between a receipts and payments account and an income and expenditure account • make adjustments for accruals, pre-payments, depreciation and the treatment of subscriptions in arrears and advance • prepare the Income and Expenditure account • prepare a Balance Sheet • close down the revenue accounts at the year end • prepare a brief summary of the accounts for the membership
5.3 Prepare a set of final accounts for a partnership	In both a manual and computerised system, be able to: • prepare a trading and profit and loss account and appropriation account from a trial balance to include adjustments • provide for the revaluation of assets and show the effect on the various capital and/or current accounts • prepare relevant partnership accounts: capital accounts and current accounts • prepare a balance sheet showing clearly the main categories of assets and liabilities • close down the revenue accounts at the year end

THE ASSESSMENT

The format of the assessment

The testing of knowledge and skills for the qualification will comprise three online assessments, all of which are taken in the candidate's home or place of work plus one assessment taken at an external ICB centre. All assessments will include testing of the Level III Bookkeeping and Accounts (Computerised) syllabus topics.

Paper BA4 – reconciliations and final accounts of a sole trader:

Home/place of work based assessment to include:

- Underpinning knowledge (5% weighting)

- Reconciliation and correction of errors (customer and supplier reconciliations, bank reconciliation, correction of errors) (15% weighting

- VAT Returns (15% weighting)

- Posting adjustments including disposal and acquisition of fixed assets (15% weighting)

- Final accounts of a sole trader (20% weighting)

- Production of final accounts of a sole trader with adjustments using a computerised package (30% weighting)

This paper must be sat first.

Paper BA5 – final accounts of a partnership

Home/place of work based covering both manual and computerised knowledge and skills assessment to include:

- Underpinning knowledge (10% weighting)

- Posting adjustments including disposal and acquisition of fixed assets (30% weighting)

- Final accounts of a partnership including the appropriation account and production of partners' current accounts (60% weighting)

Paper BA6 – final accounts of a not-for-profit organisation

Home/place of work based covering both manual and computerised knowledge and skills assessment to include:

- Underpinning knowledge (10% weighting)
- Posting adjustments including the subscriptions account and disposal and acquisition of fixed assets (30% weighting)
- Final accounts of a not-for-profit organisation (60% weighting)

These two papers can be sat in any order.

Paper BA7 – Level III External Assessment

A single assessment to be taken at an ICB assessment centre will be a mixture of multi-choice and data entry questions which will cover all elements of the syllabus.

This assessment is taken last of all.

All assessments must be successfully achieved to gain the full qualification.

Each assessment will generate a separate unit accreditation notification.

STUDY SKILLS

Preparing to study

Devise a study plan

Determine which times of the week you will study.

Split these times into sessions of at least one hour for study of new material. Any shorter periods could be used for revision or practice.

Put the times you plan to study onto a study plan for the weeks from now until the assessment and set yourself targets for each period of study – in your sessions make sure you cover the whole course, activities and the associated questions in the workbook at the back of the manual.

If you are studying more than one qualification at a time, try to vary your subjects as this can help to keep you interested and see subjects as part of wider knowledge.

When working through your course, compare your progress with your plan and, if necessary, re-plan your work (perhaps including extra sessions) or, if you are ahead, do some extra revision / practice questions.

Effective studying

Active reading

You are not expected to learn the text by rote, rather, you must understand what you are reading and be able to use it to pass the assessment and develop good practice.

A good technique is to use SQ3Rs – Survey, Question, Read, Recall, Review:

1   **Survey the chapter**

     Look at the headings and read the introduction, knowledge, skills and content, so as to get an overview of what the chapter deals with.

2   **Question**

     Whilst undertaking the survey ask yourself the questions you hope the chapter will answer for you.

3   Read

Read through the chapter thoroughly working through the activities and, at the end, making sure that you can meet the learning objectives highlighted on the first page.

4   Recall

At the end of each section and at the end of the chapter, try to recall the main ideas of the section / chapter without referring to the text. This is best done after short break of a couple of minutes after the reading stage.

5   Review

Check that your recall notes are correct.

You may also find it helpful to re-read the chapter to try and see the topic(s) it deals with as a whole.

Note taking

Taking notes is a useful way of learning, but do not simply copy out the text.

The notes must:

- be in your own words
- be concise
- cover the key points
- well organised
- be modified as you study further chapters in this text or in related ones.

Trying to summarise a chapter without referring to the text can be a useful way of determining which areas you know and which you don't.

Three ways of taking notes

1   Summarise the key points of a chapter

2   Make linear notes

A list of headings, subdivided with sub-headings listing the key points.

If you use linear notes, you can use different colours to highlight key points and keep topic areas together.

Use plenty of space to make your notes easy to use.

3   **Try a diagrammatic form**

The most common of which is a mind map.

To make a mind map, put the main heading in the centre of the paper and put a circle around it.

Draw lines radiating from this to the main sub-headings which again have circles around them.

Continue the process from the sub-headings to sub-sub-headings.

Highlighting and underlining

You may find it useful to underline or highlight key points in your study text – but do be selective.

You may also wish to make notes in the margins.

Further reading

In addition to this text, you should also refer to the ICB website for further information about your assessments.

KAPLAN PUBLISHING

Installing SAGE and company Set-up

1

CONTENTS

1   Introduction
2   Background to the business
3   Installing SAGE
4   Company set-up

1 Introduction

The aim of this manual is to guide you through the computerised accounting aspects of your ICB Level III studies.

To complete this manual you will need to have achieved ICB Level II Certificate in Bookkeeping. as well as worked through the study text for ICB Level III Manual Bookkeeping, and will need to have a copy of SAGE. There are a number of versions of SAGE available; this manual uses SAGE Instant Accounts version 19. If you have another version of SAGE, or even another accounting package, you should still be able to proceed without too much difficulty, although you may find that some of the screen-shots used in the manual differ.

The manual uses a case study approach to guide you step-by-step through the syllabus. It assumes that you are familiar with using a computerised accounting package to the standard required at ICB Level II.

2 Background to the business

The case study business used in the following chapters is Prospect Parts.

Prospect Parts is a business owned and run by Dan Matthews. It is based in Billingshire, and supplies a variety of car parts, which it buys from UK suppliers, to garages around the country on credit.

You have been recently employed as the bookkeeper of Prospect Parts. The business currently uses a manual bookkeeping system, and Dan would like to swap to a computerised system in order to make the business more efficient.

Today's date is 31st December 2013 – the last day of the business's accounting period.

3 Installing SAGE

When you install SAGE v19 for the first time, you should see this screen:

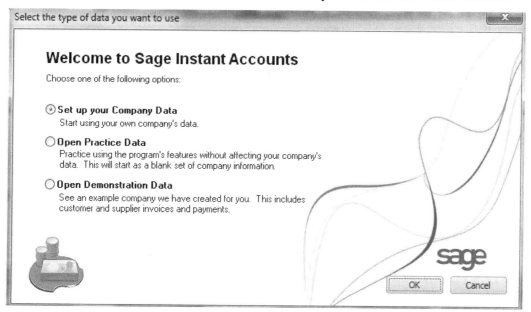

As you are entering data for a new company in this case study, you will need to make sure you check the "Set up your Company Data" option, and the select "ok".

You should then see the screen below:

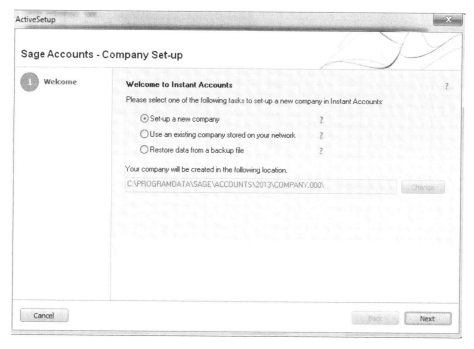

This gives you the option of setting up a new company or uploading existing data. For the purposes of this case study, you will be setting up a new company, so you will need to select the "Set-up a new company" option shown above.

Once you have set up the new company details, SAGE will default to that every time you open the program.

4 Company set-up

You will now need to enter the company details into SAGE. These will appear on the various reports you will need to produce. You will also need to enter your company's financial year start date: SAGE will use this information when generating your annual accounts. You are guided through the set-up process by SAGE's ActiveSetup wizard, which shows the following steps:

Step 2: Company Details

The data for the company in this case study, Prospect Parts, is given below:

Business Name:	Prospect Parts
Business Address:	15 Prospect Street
	Greentown
	Billingshire
	BE2 4RP
Telephone:	0123 4567890
Fax:	0123 4567890
Email:	info@prospectparts.boonet.co.uk
Website:	www.prospectparts.co.uk
VAT Number:	567 2345 01
Financial Year:	1st January – 31st December

Entering these details on SAGE, you will see the following screen:

Once you have checked these details, you can click on "Next" to move on the next screen.

Step 3: Business Type

You can choose from a number of business types on this screen: for this case study, you are preparing accounts for a sole trader, and need to make sure you select this option. This will ensure SAGE creates nominal codes which are specifically designed for a sole trader.

Step 4: Financial Year

Here, you will need to enter the month when your company financial year begins: as Prospect Parts' financial year ends on 31st December 2013, this will be January 2013.

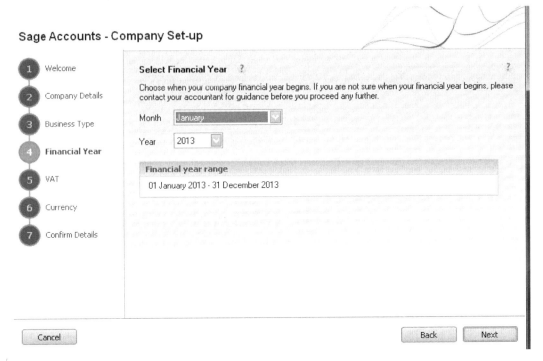

Step 5: VAT

Prospect Parts is registered for VAT, so you will need to enter the VAT registration details in this screen.

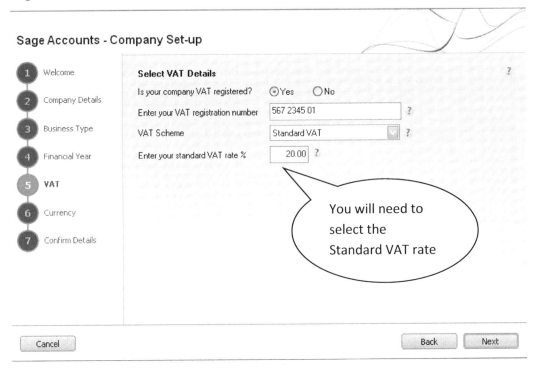

Step 6: Currency

You will now need to set up the currency details for the company. Prospect Parts trades within the UK, and so you need to select Pound Sterling as the currency SAGE will use.

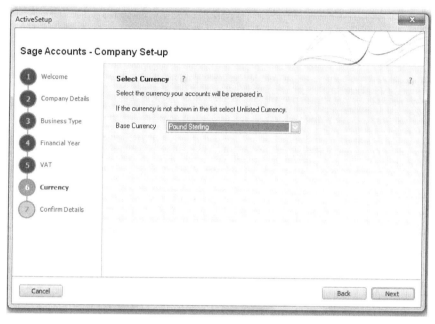

Step 7: Confirm Details

This final screen in the set-up wizard allows you to check the accuracy of the company data you have entered, and then go back and amend details as necessary. When you are happy this is all correct, you can click on "Create" to finish the company set-up process.

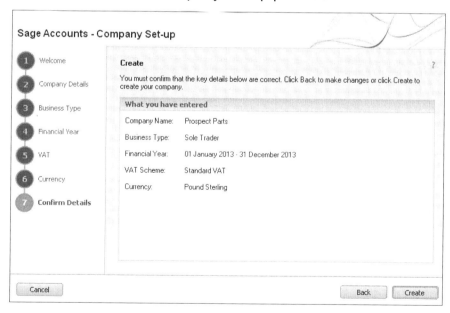

Your business has now been successfully set up and you are ready to move on to the exercises in the following chapters.

A reminder of the basics

CONTENTS
1   Dates
2   Correcting errors
3   Adding and editing nominal codes
4   Exporting files
5   Rebuilding new data

1 Dates

Each time you open SAGE, it will use your computer's internal clock to set the default date and time.

When you are working through the practice case studies and mock assessment in this study text, it is a good idea to override this and enter a date in line with the material on which you are working. This will save you time as otherwise you will need to amend the date each time you enter a transaction.

To change the default date from today's real date, you will need to select "Settings" along the top toolbar in SAGE and then "Change program date".

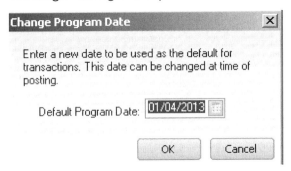

You can now enter the date required by the example you are working on. SAGE will use this as the default date until the next time you open the program, at which point the default date will revert to the real date once again.

2 Correcting errors

If you enter a transaction incorrectly on SAGE, you will need to correct the error by posting a correcting journal, using the Journal Entry icon in the Company module:

To correct an entry posted to the Creditors control account and the Debtors control account, you will need to use the Corrections function within the Task module. This will allow you to either delete or amend the incorrect transaction.

3 Adding and editing nominal codes

It is important that you use an appropriate nominal code for every transaction you enter on SAGE. This will ensure that the accounts you produce are meaningful and relevant to the business.

If there is not a suitable nominal code already set up in the default chart of accounts on SAGE, you can either edit an existing code, or add an additional code.

Editing an existing code

To edit an existing nominal code, simply double-click on the relevant nominal code heading within the nominal ledger in the "Company" module.

The nominal record for that particular code will then be displayed: you can amend the name of the account by entering the new name in the "Name" box.

In the example below N/C0030 Office Equipment has been renamed "Computer Equipment":

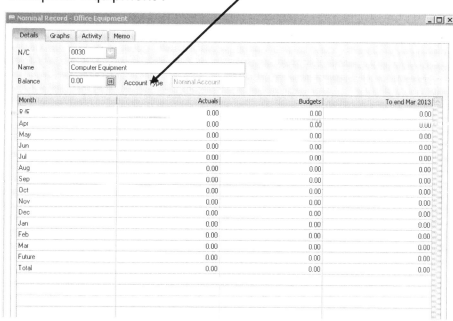

You will then need to select "Yes" to save the changes made.

Adding a new nominal code

You can also add a new nominal code on SAGE: remember that you need to choose a nominal code in the correct range in SAGE so that the new nominal account appears in the correct section of the Balance Sheet or Profit and Loss Account.

You can check where a particular range of nominal codes will appear in the Balance Sheet or Profit and Loss Account by selecting the "Chart of Accounts" option within the "Company" module.

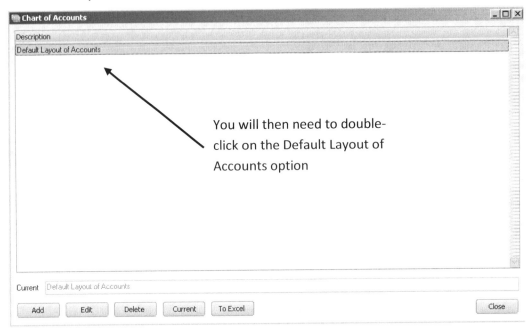

You will then need to double-click on the Default Layout of Accounts option

You should then select either the Profit and Loss tab or the Balance Sheet tab to see how nominal codes are allocated under each heading. When setting up a new nominal code, you should take care to select one that will appear under the correct heading in the Profit and Loss Account or the Balance Sheet.

In this screen you can also edit the wording of the headings that will appear within the Profit and Loss Account and Balance Sheet, as shown below.

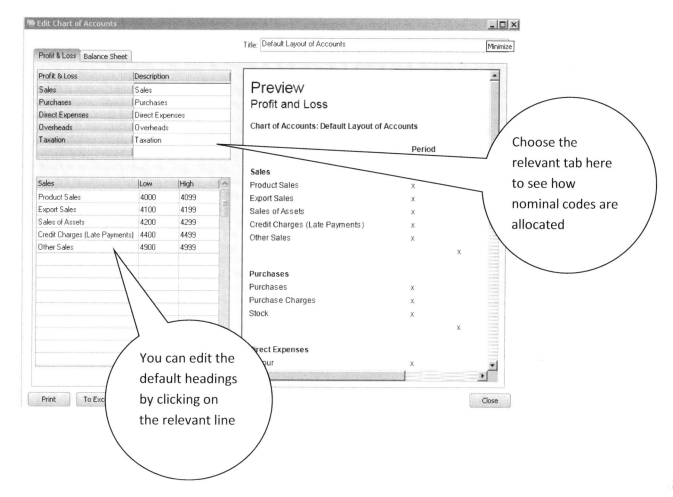

Once you have identified a suitable new nominal code to use, you can add this to the chart of accounts by clicking on the "New Nominal" option within the "Company" module. Remember to click on "Save" to save any changes made.

4 Exporting files

You can export files from SAGE in various formats, including as a pdf and an Excel file.

To export a file from SAGE, such as a Trial Balance, select "Export" along the top toolbar of the file. You will then see a drop down menu from which you can select the correct format.

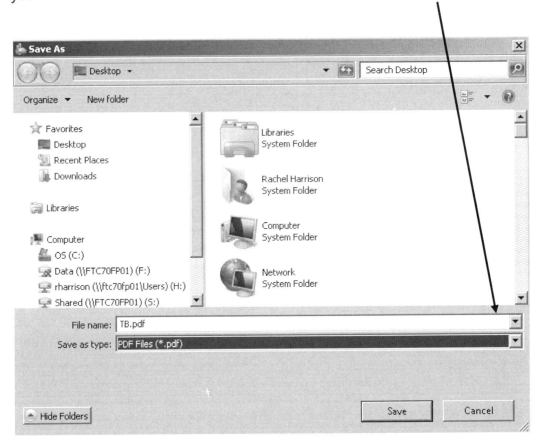

5 Rebuilding new data

Each time you work through a new practice example on SAGE, you will need to erase the existing data files and start from scratch. You should always back up your existing work before doing this in case you need to access it again at a later date.

To rebuild new data on SAGE you will need to follow these steps:

1 Click on "File" and then "Maintenance" along the top toolbar.

2 Select "Rebuild new data"

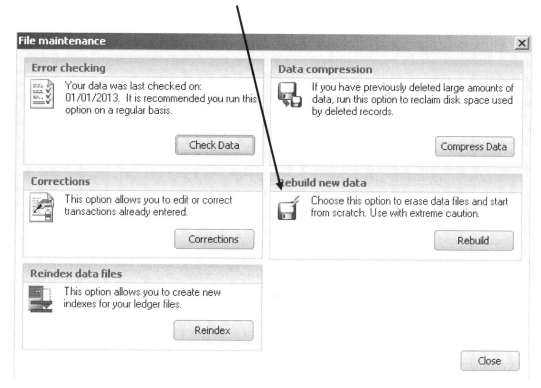

3 Uncheck all of the boxes, and select the type of business you now want to set up on SAGE: in this case, a Sole Trader has been selected. SAGE will generate a chart of accounts based on the business type selected here.

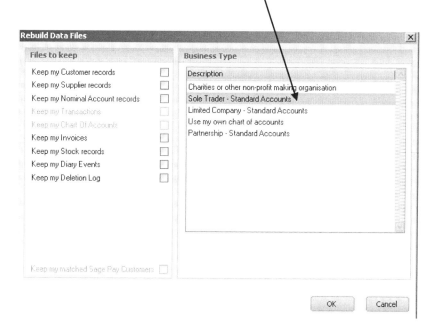

You then need to select "OK" and enter the new financial year start date for the business you will be working on.

Note that once you have completed this, you will need to update the Company details, such as name and business address, within the "Company Preferences" option in the "Settings" tab on the top toolbar.

Posting opening balances on SAGE

3

CONTENTS

1 Introduction

Now that you have set up the company details on SAGE, you are ready to enter the customer and supplier data, and the opening trial balance.

2 Customer data

Prospect Parts has three customers with outstanding balances at 31st December 2013. Their details are shown below, together with the outstanding invoices at 31 December 2013.

Red Motors Ltd   **A/c Ref : RED001**
2 Red Street
Redtown
Redshire
RE1 7YT

Outstanding invoices at 31st December 2013:

Invoice no 2531   30.11.13 £252.56

Invoice no 2640   10.12.13 £769.88

Credit Terms: **Payment in 28 days**   **Credit Limit £5000**

Green Motors Ltd   **A/c Ref : GRE001**
3 Green Street
Greentown
Greenshire
GR8 5GH

Outstanding invoices at 31st December 2013

Invoice no 1680 17.02.13   £526.13

Credit Terms: **Payment in 28 days**   **Credit Limit £1000**

Yellow Motors Ltd
13 Yellow Street
Yellowtown
Yellowshire
YE23 5HY

A/c Ref : YEL001

Outstanding invoices at 31st December 2013

Invoice no 2702 28.12.13 £452.10

Invoice no 2705 29.12.13 £500.26

Credit Terms: **Payment in 28 days**

Credit Limit £1500

You will need to enter these customers on to SAGE before posting the opening trial balance.

Step 1

Click on the "New Customer" option shown in the Tasks panel.

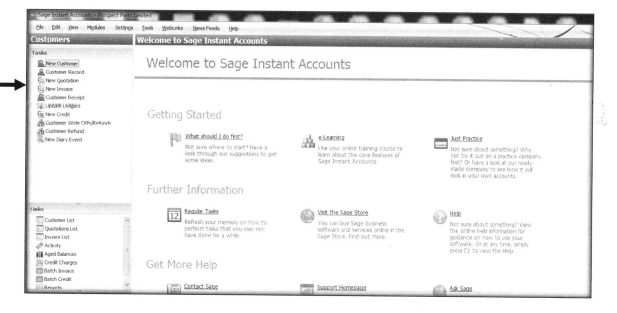

Step 2

Enter the customer address details and account reference.

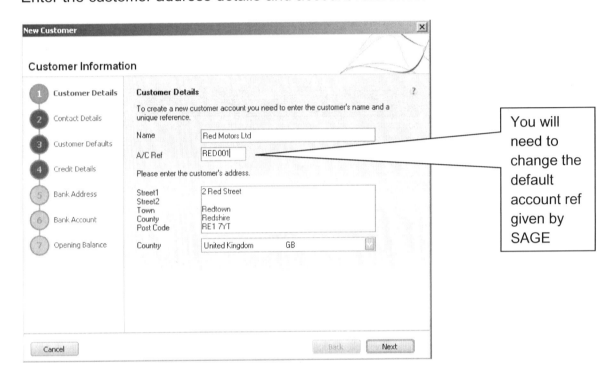

You will need to change the default account ref given by SAGE

Step 3

Enter any customer contact details: you can leave this blank as none are given in this case study.

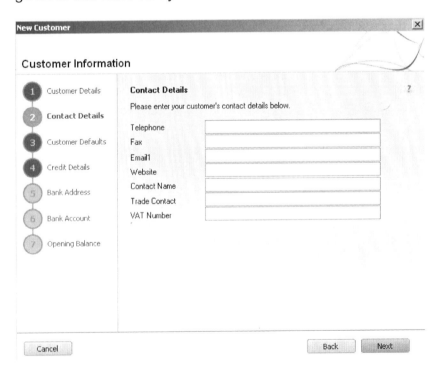

Step 4

Select your customer default information. The nominal code of 4000 and the tax code of T1 20% should be already selected by SAGE.

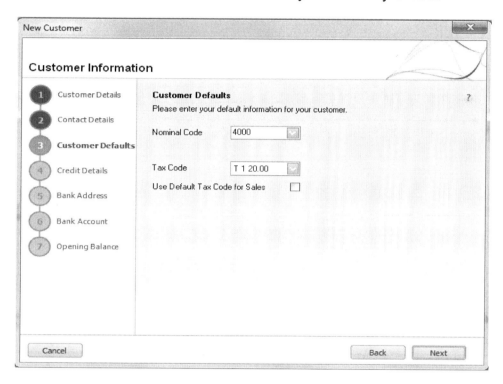

Step 5

Enter the customer credit details.

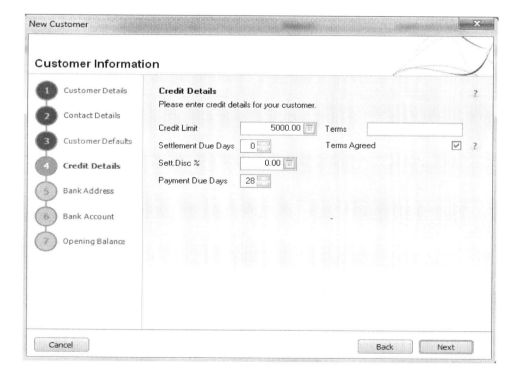

Step 6

The next two screens ask you to enter your customer bank details: again, you can leave these blank as none are given for this case study.

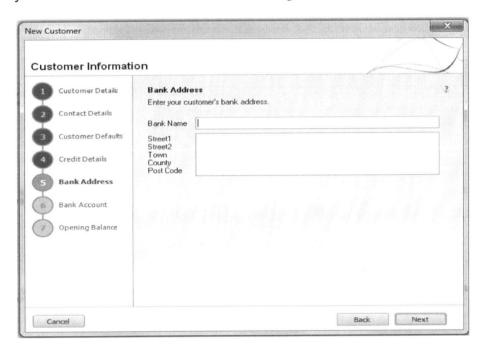

Step 7

You can now enter the opening balance for the customer.

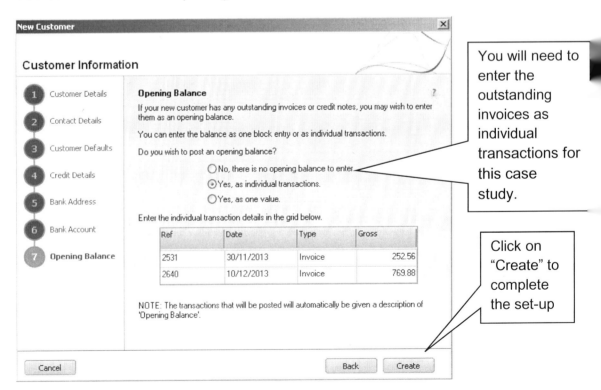

You will need to enter the outstanding invoices as individual transactions for this case study.

Click on "Create" to complete the set-up

You will now need to enter the other two customer details in the same way.

When you have completed this, your Customers screen should look like this:

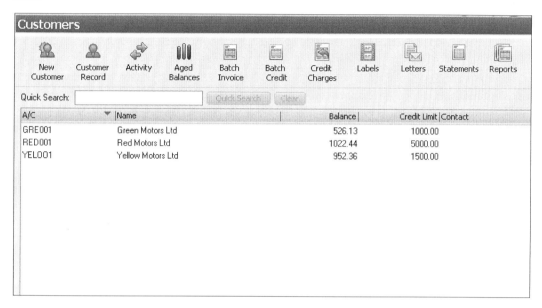

3 Supplier data

Prospect Parts has an outstanding balance with three of its suppliers at the 31st December 2013. The details of these are shown below.

You will need to enter these details by opening the Suppliers screen, and selecting the "New Supplier" option shown below. The set-up process follows the same steps as the Customer set-up process you have just followed.

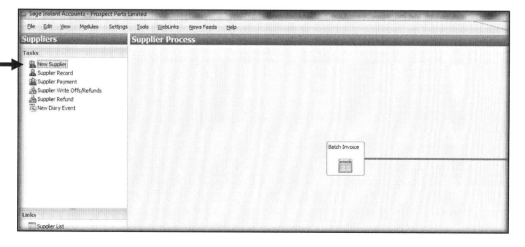

Exercise

Using the New Supplier Process, enter the details of Prospect Part's three suppliers shown below.

Pink Tyres Ltd   A/c Ref : PIN001
2 Pink Street
Pinktown
Pinkshire
PK1 7YT

Outstanding invoices at 31st December 2013

Invoice no 4598 28.12.13 £1800.00

Credit Terms: **Payment in 28 days**   **Credit Limit £5000**

Blue Exhausts Ltd   A/c Ref : BLU001
2 Blue Street
Bluetown
Blueshire
BL1 7YT

Outstanding invoices at 31st December 2013

Invoice no 34146 20.12.13 £658.45

Invoice no 35322 27.12.13 £572.42

Credit Terms: **Payment in 28 days**   **Credit Limit £5000**

Mauve Motors Ltd
2 Mauve Street
Mauvetown
Mauveshire
MA1 7YT

A/c Ref : MAU001

Outstanding invoices at 31st December 2013

Invoice no 675 2.12.13 £75.00

Invoice no 712 12.12.13 £127.25

Credit Terms: **Payment in 28 days**

Credit Limit £1000

Once you have entered these details, your screen should like this:

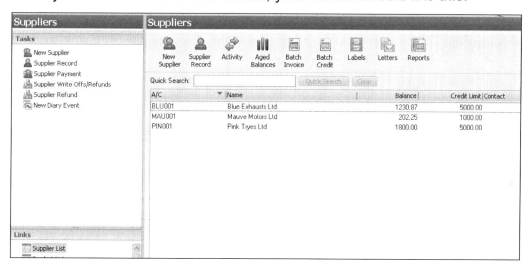

4 Entering the opening Trial Balance

You are now ready to post the opening trial balance of Prospect Parts on SAGE. Remember that you will need to use the date at which you first started using SAGE to record transactions for the company, i.e. 31st December 2013.

The list of opening balances for Prospect Parts is given below.

Don't forget that you will not need to enter the balances for the Debtors control account and the Creditors control account, as these are the totals of the customers' and suppliers' accounts which you have just entered above.

Prospect Parts

Opening Balances

	Nominal code	Debit	Credit
Office Equipment (at cost)	0030	3250.00	
Depreciation (Office Equipment)	0031		1750.00
Motor vehicles (at cost)	0050	26500.00	
Depreciation (Motor Vehicles)	0051		4500.00
Stock (as at 1st January 2013)	1001	900.00	
Debtors Control Account	1100	2500.93	
Prepayments	1103	250.00	
Bank	1200	1726.29	
Petty Cash	1230	300.00	
Creditors Control Account	2100		3233.12
Accruals	2109		200.00
VAT Liability	2202		947.50
Capital account	3000		15715.83
Drawings	3050	5720.00	
Sales – Tyres	4000		47224.46
Sales – Exhausts	4001		32643.27
Sales – Other	4002		9456.87
Purchases – Tyres	5000	32534.36	
Purchases – Exhausts	5001	17668.89	
Purchases – Other	5002	6879.21	
Gross wages	7000	13520.65	
Rent	7100	850.00	
General Rates	7103	845.62	
Miscellaneous Motor Expenses	7304	1024.36	
Telephone	7550	546.31	
Sundry expenses	8250	654.43	
		115671.05	**115671.05**

Entering an Opening Balance in SAGE

On the main screen, you will need to select the "Company" module.

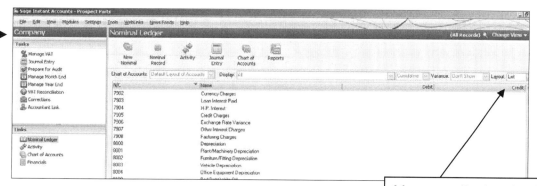

You can display the full list of the nominal codes for the company by selecting "List" from the Layout menu

You will then need to highlight the nominal code for which you want to enter an opening balance. The first account on Prospect Parts' opening trial balance is Office Equipment, with a debit balance of £3250. From the list of nominal codes, you can see that you need to enter this opening balance in account number **0030**.

Double-click on this account, and then click on the "Opening Balance" icon.

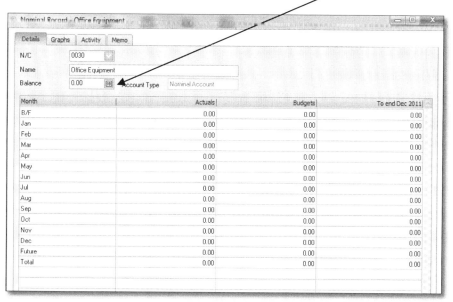

You can now complete the opening balance set-up for this nominal account, making sure that the date box is set to 31st December 2013, and then click on "Save".

Adding and Amending Nominal Codes in SAGE

You can find a reminder of how to add and amend nominal codes in SAGE in chapter 2 of this book.

Exercise

You should now be able to enter the opening balances for each of the accounts.

Important

1   You do not need to enter opening balances for the Debtors Control Account and the Creditors Control Account. These represent the total amount owed to us (debtors) and the total amount we owe (creditors), made up of all of the individual balances you entered earlier. These control account balances are calculated automatically by SAGE and you do not enter them again.

2   Take care to enter each balance correctly and on the correct debit or credit side.

5   Checking the opening Trial Balance

Before you continue to enter transactions for Prospect Parts, you should make sure that you have entered the opening trial balance correctly.

To do this, you will need to view the trial balance as at 31st December 2013 and check all of the account balances are correct, and that no suspense account has been created by SAGE to balance the debits and credits you have entered.

In order to view the trial balance, you will need to select the Trial Balance icon in the Company Financials screen:

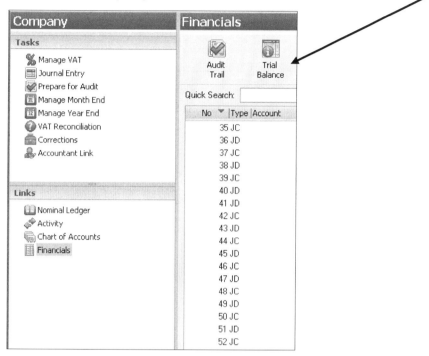

You will then need to select the "Preview" option to view the trial balance on screen, making sure that the date is set to December 2013 in the "Criteria Values" box, and then click "OK".

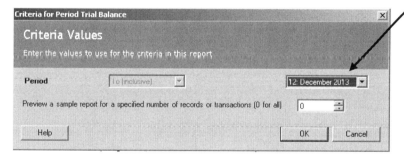

You should see that your trial balance is the same as the one below, and that the total of both the debit and credit columns adds up to £115,671.05.

If there are any errors in your trial balance at this stage, or if a suspense account has been created by SAGE as your debit and credit columns do not balance due to a mistake you have made, then you can correct these following the steps set out in chapter 2.

Date: 14/01/2014   **Prospect Parts**   Page: 1
Time: 13:26:50   **Period Trial Balance**

To Period: Month 12, December 2013

N/C	Name	Debit	Credit
0030	Office Equipment	3,250.00	
0031	Office Equipment Depreciation		1,750.00
0050	Motor Vehicles	26,500.00	
0051	Motor Vehicles Depreciation		4,500.00
1001	Stock	900.00	
1100	Debtors Control Account	2,500.93	
1103	Prepayments	250.00	
1200	Bank Current Account	1,726.29	
1230	Petty Cash	300.00	
2100	Creditors Control Account		3,233.12
2109	Accruals		200.00
2202	VAT Liability		947.50
3000	Capital		15,715.83
3050	Drawings	5,720.00	
4000	Sales - Tyres		47,224.46
4001	Sales - Exhausts		32,643.27
4002	Sales - Other		9,456.87
5000	Purchases - Tyres	32,534.36	
5001	Pucrhases - Exhausts	17,668.89	
5002	Purchases - Other	6,879.21	
7000	Gross Wages	13,520.65	
7100	Rent	850.00	
7103	General Rates	845.62	
7304	Miscellaneous Motor Expenses	1,024.36	
7550	Telephone	546.31	
8250	Sundry Expenses	654.43	
	Totals:	115,671.05	115,671.05

Notice that no suspense account has been created by SAGE and so the debit and credit columns both balance.

Stock

CONTENTS

1 Introduction

Many businesses will hold some unsold stock at the end of their financial year. This could be in the form of raw materials, work-in-progress, and/or finished goods.

An adjustment in respect of closing stock is made to the financial statements at the financial year-end. This ensures that any unsold stock can be carried forward in the Balance Sheet to match with future revenues, and is applying the accruals concept.

In order to adjust for closing stock in SAGE, you will first of all need to calculate an accurate closing stock value, based on the business's end of year stock take.

2 Methods of valuation

Current accounting standards state that stock should be valued at **the lower of cost and net realisable value,** and that stock should be valued **on a line by line basis.**

Cost

The cost of stock is defined as the cost incurred in the normal course of business in bringing an item to its present location or condition.

There are several ways allowed of valuing stock:

- Actual unit cost
- First-in, First-out (FIF0)
- Weighted average cost (AVCO)

Net realisable value

The net realisable value of an item of stock is the estimated proceeds from selling it, less all further costs to completion and costs incurred in marketing, selling and distribution.

KAPLAN PUBLISHING

Weighted Average Cost (AVCO)

The AVCO method of stock valuation is used where there are a large number of identical items held for which it would be impossible or impractical to calculate an individual cost. A common example is grain held in a bin.

The average price of a unit is calculated as a weighted average, and is recalculated after each receipt of goods.

First-in, First-out (FIFO)

This method assumes goods are sold or used in production in the order in which they are purchased. The closing value of inventory using FIFO will be the cost of the items most recently purchased/produced.

Example

A business commenced trading on 1st January, and has made purchases as follows:

Month	No of units	Cost per unit £	Value £
January	200	5	1,000
February	300	6	1,800
May	100	5.50	550
September	400	5.75	2,300
November	200	6	1,200
Total	1,200		6,850

The business sold 500 units in June.

Requirement

(a)   What is the value of closing stock using the FIFO method?

(b)   What is the value of closing stock using the AVCO method?

Note: There will be some rounding differences in your calculations, as the average costs below are taken to 3 decimal places.

Solution

(a)   There are 700 units (1200 units purchased less 500 units sold) in stock at 31st December. These will be valued assuming the oldest goods are sold first. Therefore, the business has sold the 200 units purchased in January and the 300 units purchased in February first, which leaves it with the following items in stock:

No of units	Cost per unit £	Total cost £
100	5.50	550
400	5.75	2,300
200	6	1,200
Closing stock cost		**4,050**

(b)   There are 700 units in stock at 31st December, which will be valued according to the weighted average cost of the goods purchased.

Month	No of units	Weighted Average Cost £	Total Stock Value £
January	200	5	1,000
February	300	6	1,800
Total	500	5.6	2,800
May	100	5.50	550
Total	600	5.583	3,350
June	(500)	5.583	(2,791.50)
Total	100	5.583	558.50
September	400	5.75	2,300
Total	500	5.72	2858.50
November	200	6	1,200
Closing stock cost	700	5.798	4058.50

Case Study

(a)   Prospect Parts uses the AVCO method of stock valuation.

From the Trial Balance in chapter 3, you can see that the company had opening stock with a weighted average cost of £900 as at 1st January 2013. This was the cost of 20 M-brand tyres.

Movements of the stock of M-brand tyres were as follows:

Purchases: Month	No of Units	Cost per unit	
Op. bal.	20	£ 45	= 900
February	30	50	1500
May	20	47	940
November	25	46	1150

Sales: Month	No of units	
January	15	= 675
March	20	
September	30	

Requirement

Calculate the value of stock at 31st December 2013 which will be shown in Prospect Part Ltd's financial statements.

Jan. —   5 × 45 = - 225
Fab   + 30 × 50 = 1500
            35 × 49,29 = 1725,15
March —   20 × 49,29 = - 985.80
          15 × 49,29 = 739.35
May   20 × 47 = 940
          35 × 47.98 = 1679.35
Sept. —   30 × 47.98 = 1439.40
          5 × 47.99 = 239.95
Nov. + 25 × 46 = 1150
          30
                    = 1389.95

Solution

Note: There are some rounding differences in these calculations, as the average costs are taken to 3 decimal places.

Month	No of units	Weighted Average Cost £	Total Stock Value £
Opening stock	20	45	900
January	(15)	45	(675)
Total	5	45	225
February	30	50	1,500
Total	35	49.286	1,725
March	(20)	49.286	(986)
Total	15	49.286	739
May	20	47	940
Total	35	47.98	1,679
September	(30)	47.98	(1,439)
Total	5	47.98	240
November	25	46	1,150
Closing stock cost	30	46.33	**1,390**

3 Adjusting for closing stock in SAGE

You can see from the exercise above that Prospect Parts' closing stock has increased to £1,390 from the opening stock value of £900. This means the level of stock has risen by £490.

This has an effect on the both the Profit and Loss Account and the Balance Sheet.

The cost of goods sold, shown in the Profit and Loss Account, will be affected as **Cost of goods sold = Opening stock N/C5200 + Purchases – Closing stock N/C5201.**

The Balance Sheet will be affected as stock N/C1001 is a current asset.

To account for the closing stock in SAGE, you will need to enter two journals:

- The first journal transfers the opening stock asset of £900 from the Balance Sheet N/C1001 to the opening stock account N/C5200 in the Profit and Loss Account. Note that where there is no opening stock, you will not need to enter this journal.

- The second journal records the value of the closing stock at the end of the year in both the Profit and Loss Account closing stock account N/C5201 and the Balance Sheet stock account N/C1001.

You will need to open up a journal from the Company Nominal Ledger screen:

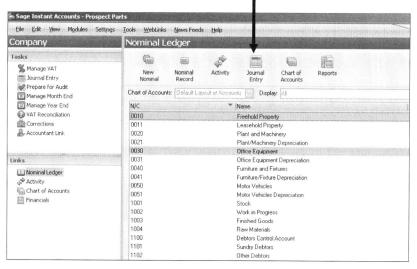

Firstly, transfer the opening stock from the Balance Sheet to the opening stock account in the Profit and Loss Account:

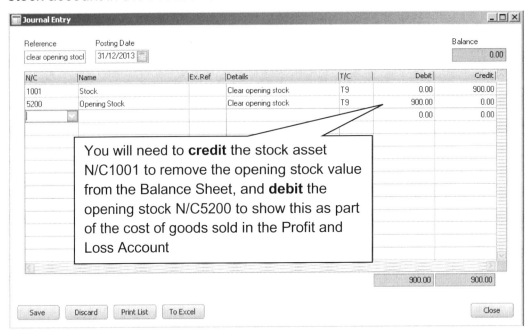

Then, enter the closing stock value as at 31st December 2013 in both the Balance sheet stock account, and the Profit and Loss Account closing stock account:

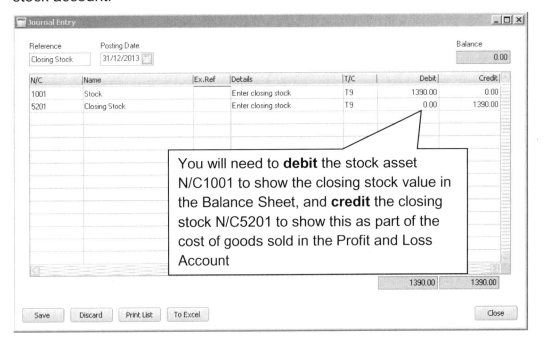

You should now check that your entries have been recorded correctly:

The Trial Balance will show a closing stock figure in the Balance Sheet stock account N/C1001 of £1,390, as per Prospect Parts' stock-take. If your figure is not correct, check you have correctly transferred the opening stock figure to the Profit and Loss Account.

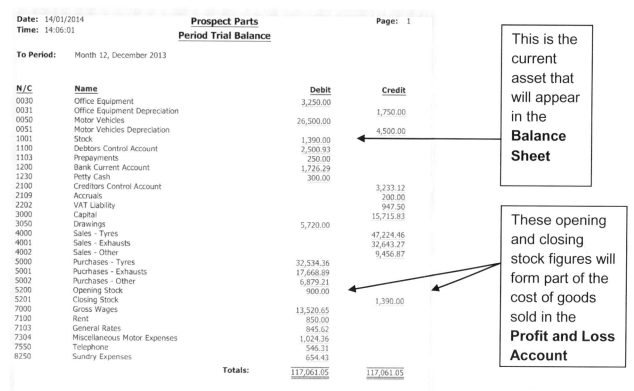

The extracts below show you how the closing stock will appear in the Balance Sheet and the Profit and Loss Account. You can view these by choosing the Profit and Loss and Balance Sheet options within the Company Financials Module on SAGE.

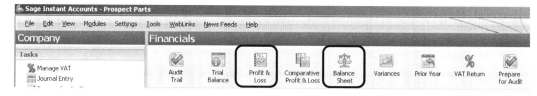

Extract from the Balance Sheet

Current Assets				
Stock	1,390.00		1,390.00	
Debtors	2,750.93		2,750.93	
Deposits and Cash	300.00		300.00	
Bank Account	1,726.29		1,726.29	
		6,167.22		6,167.22

Extract from the Profit and Loss Account

Purchases				
Purchases	57,082.46		57,082.46	
Stock	(490.00)		(490.00)	
		56,592.46		56,592.46

You should note that the Profit and Loss Account will show the net stock movement at the year end, so here there is a £490 increase in Prospect Parts' stock value.

It will help you to remember that Opening Stock + Purchases – Closing Stock = Cost of Goods Sold.

In the case study you are working on, this is: £900 + £57,082.46 – £1,390 = £56,592.46.

Bank reconciliation

5

CONTENTS

1 Introduction

A useful exercise for all businesses to undertake on a regular basis is to reconcile their bank account. In essence this means checking the company's own records with the bank statement produced and sent to them by their bank.

Dan asks you to enter the following items on SAGE before performing the bank reconciliation.

Receipts

- 31/12/2013: Cheque for £452.10 from Yellow Motors Ltd

Payments

- 30/12/2013: Cheque number 250 paid to Mauve Motors Ltd: £75.00

- 31/12/2013: Cheque number 251 paid to Tiny Telecoms Ltd to pay the phone bill: £75.72

You will need to enter the receipt from Yellow Motors Ltd using the Customer Receipts function:

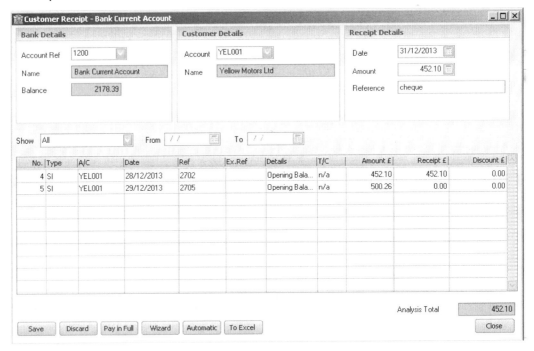

The payment to Mauve Motors Ltd should then be entered using the Supplier Payments function:

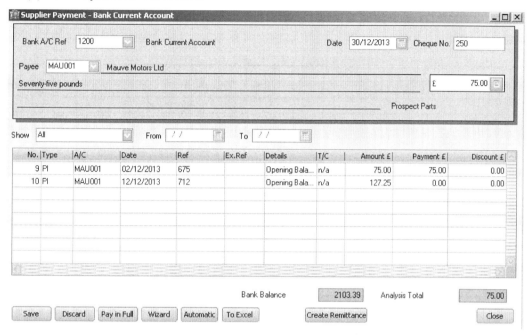

Finally, the cheque payment to Tiny Telecoms Ltd should be entered using the Bank Payments function:

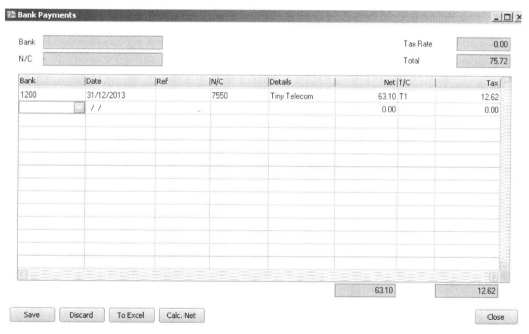

2   Difference between the bank statement and the bank control account

Prospect Parts received the following statement from their bank.

STATEMENT			
Account number		Date 31/12/2013	
Sort code		Statement No: 49	
Date	Payments	Receipts	Balance
28/12/13 Op Bal			1726.29
31/12/13 Direct Credit: Red Motors Ltd		252.56	1978.85
31/12/13 Interest		8.17	1987.02
31/12/13 Bank Charges	14.60		1972.42

The bank statement will rarely agree exactly with the company's own records, for three reasons:

1   Items on the Bank Statement not yet recorded in SAGE

There may be some items on the bank statement which do not yet appear in the company's records. Here, there is interest which has been credited to the business bank account of £8.17, a direct credit of £252.56 from a customer, and also bank charges of £14.60 which have been debited from the account. It is likely that the company would not know the exact amount or date of these receipts to/payments from the bank account until the statement is actually received.

Similarly, you should always check that all standing orders/direct debits/BACS transfers etc. have been fully recorded in the company's records. In this case, there is a direct credit from Red Motors Ltd which has not yet been posted to SAGE.

Remember that a 'recurring item' can be set up within SAGE but that these must still be posted.

Discrepancies of this nature between the bank statement and the company's own records should be dealt with by updating the company's records.

You should now enter a **bank payment** to deal with the bank charges and a **bank receipt** to deal with the interest received and the receipt from the customer.

Here is the screen for the **bank payment**. Remember there is no VAT on bank charges (or interest) and so the VAT code should be set to T2 (Exempt).

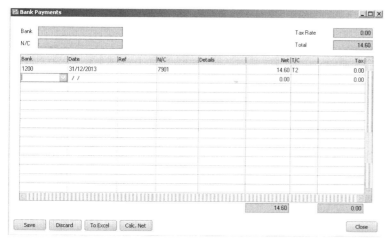

Here is the screen for the **bank receipt** of the interest. Note that there was no Nominal Code for *Interest Received* and so a new N/C has been created (N/C 4906).

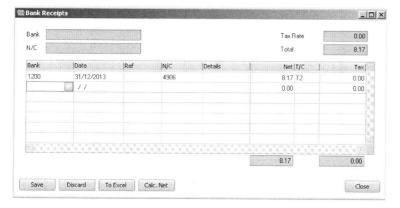

You will now need to enter the receipt from Red Motors Ltd, using the customer receipt function:

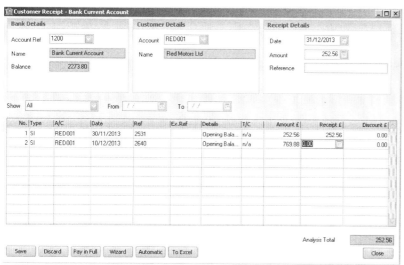

2 Timing Differences

This is a very common cause of discrepancies between the bank statement and the company's own records. Timing differences occur because the company will generally update its records before the bank has had the opportunity to process all transactions.

Imagine the scenario where a company writes a cheque to a supplier on 1st March. The accounts clerk is likely to update the company's records (i.e. SAGE) on that day. However, if the cheque was produced late in the afternoon it may not actually be posted until the following day and may not arrive at the supplier's address until two or three days after that. Weekends and public holidays can delay this further. It may then not be banked immediately by the supplier; it may take them two or three days to actually bank the cheque in their own branch. The cheque must then go through the banks' clearing system which may take three-five working days. Therefore the funds associated with that cheque (written on 1st March) may not actually be cleared out of the bank account until say 10th March or maybe later.

If a bank statement is sent to the company in this time it will not show the cheque payment, as it will not have been fully processed at the time the statement is produced. It will, however, have been recorded in the company's own accounts.

It is important therefore to undergo a process of bank reconciliation regularly to ensure that the only differences between the bank statement and the company's own records are caused by these timing differences (which can easily be accounted for), and not by the third reason for discrepancies, which is error.

3 Errors

It is perfectly possible for either the bank or (more likely) the company to have made an error in the course of producing their figures. You would therefore have to undertake further investigations into the cause of the error and then to correct it appropriately.

3 Performing a bank reconciliation using SAGE

From the **BANK** Module select the appropriate bank account and then click on the ⚖ button.

Reconcile

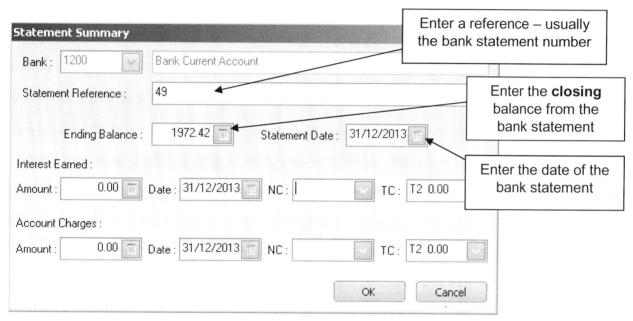

This screen allows you to enter the summary of your Bank Statement. Notice that you can also enter the interest earned and any bank charges directly via this screen as well (rather than entering them separately as bank payments and receipts as you did earlier).

The top half of this "Reconcile" screen shows transactions already entered on SAGE in N/C1200.

The bottom half of the screen shows items that you have matched to entries on the actual bank statement received from your bank.

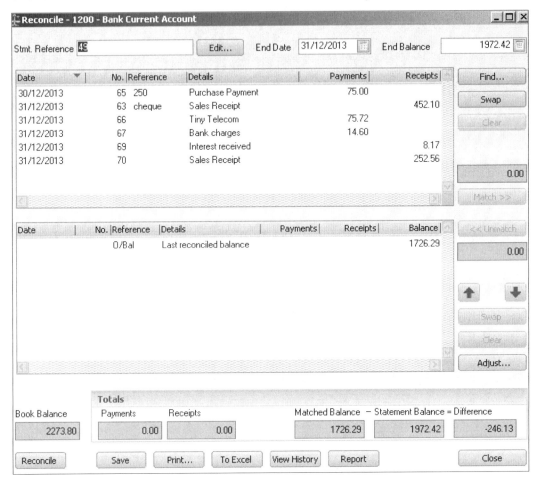

You now use this screen to 'match' the entries on your bank statement with the entries in SAGE. You do this by highlighting each entry in the Unmatched Items section and then pressing the | Match >> | button.

ONLY match the items that appear on your bank statement

You should find the following items on the bank statement and show them as 'matched'

Bank interest of £8.17

Bank charges of £14.60

Direct Credit from Red Motors Ltd of £252.56

Once you have matched all items they will appear in the 'Matched Against Statement' box as shown below:

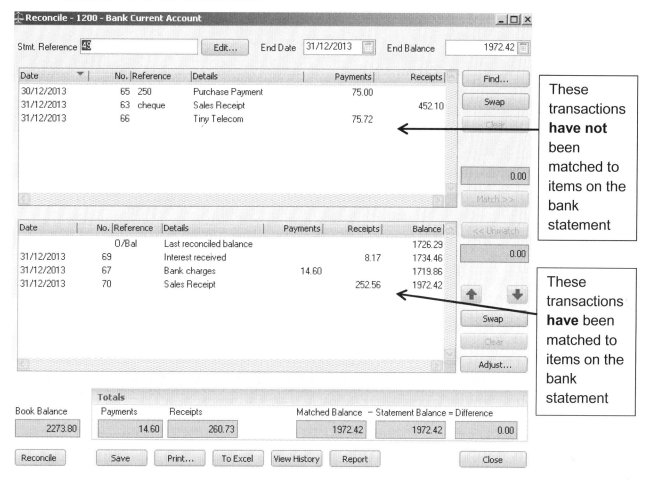

You can see here that the items which appear on the bank statement have now been matched. The matched balance now equals the statement balance and therefore the difference is zero. This is what you should be aiming for.

You should now press the [Reconcile] button to complete the process.

4 Reports

Once you have reconciled the bank statement you should produce the following reports from within Bank Reports section.

Bank Reconciled Transactions shows the list of matched and reconciled items within SAGE. (Contained in the Reconciled Transactions folder.)

Unreconciled Payments (contained in the Unreconciled transactions folder) shows the list of unreconciled payments – these are the payments that you have recorded in SAGE but which do not yet appear on the latest bank statement.

Unreconciled Receipts (also contained in the Unreconciled transactions folder) shows the list of unreconciled receipts – these are the receipts that you have recorded in SAGE but which do not yet appear on the latest bank statement.

You should produce and print each of these reports now.

Bank Reconciled Transactions Report

Date: 14/01/2014   **Prospect Parts**   **Page:** 1
Time: 15:21:35   **Bank Reconciled Transactions**

Bank Reconciled On: 31/12/2013

No	Type	Date	A/C	N/C	Dept	Ref	Details	Net	Tax	T/C
23	JD	31/12/2013	1200	1200	0	O/Bal	Opening Balance	1,726.29	0.00	T9
67	BP	31/12/2013	1200	7901	0		bank charges	14.60	0.00	T2
68	BR	31/12/2013	1200	4906	0			8.17	0.00	T2
70	SR	31/12/2013	RED001	1200	0	Direct credit	Sales Receipt	252.56	0.00	T9

Unreconciled Payments Report

Date: 14/01/2014   **Prospect Parts**   **Page:** 1
Time: 16:01:52   **Unreconciled Payments**

Date From: 01/01/1980   **Bank From:** 1200
DateTo: 31/12/2019   **Bank To:** 1200

Transaction From: 1
Transaction To: 99,999,999

Bank: 1200   **Bank Account Name:** Bank Current Account   **Currency:** Pound Sterling

No	Type	Date	Ref	Details	Amount £
72	PP	30/12/2013	250	Purchase Payment	75.00
73	BP	31/12/2013		Tiny Telecom	75.72
				Total £	150.72

Unreconciled Receipts Report

Date: 14/01/2014				**Prospect Parts**		**Page:** 1	
Time: 16:03:53				**Unreconciled Receipts**			

Date From:	01/01/1980	**Bank From:**	1200
DateTo:	31/12/2019	**Bank To:**	1200

Transaction From: 1
Transaction To: 99,999,999

Bank: 1200   **Bank Account Name:** Bank Current Account   **Currency:** Pound Sterling

No	Type	Date	Ref	Details	Amount £
71	SR	31/12/20	cheque	Sales Receipt	452.10
				Total £	452.10

These unreconciled payments and receipts will appear on future bank statements, when they will then be matched in a future reconciliation.

Reconciling the sales and purchases ledgers

CONTENTS

1 Introduction
2 Reconciling the sales ledger
3 Identifying errors
4 Reconciling the purchases ledger

1 Introduction

The debtors control account is used to record any sales invoices, credit notes and receipts from customers. It essentially summarises the balances contained in the sales ledger to show one overall total for outstanding trade debtors at a given date.

Similarly the creditors control account is used to record any purchase invoices, credit notes and payments to suppliers. This will summarise the balances contained in the purchases ledger to again show one overall total for outstanding trade creditors at a given date.

To check for any errors that may have arisen in the sales and purchases ledgers, it is important to check on a regular basis that the balances shown on these ledgers both tally with the overall balances shown on the relevant control accounts.

2 Reconciling the sales ledger

The sales ledger shows the amounts due from individual customers at a given date. SAGE allows you to view this information as either a detailed report showing the individual transactions which make up the total customer balance, or as a summary report which simply shows the total amount owed by each customer. These reports can be viewed using the Reports function within the Customers module.

Sales invoices, credit notes and receipts will be entered on SAGE using the New Invoice, Customer Receipts, and New Credit functions in the Customers module shown below. These transactions will be automatically entered by SAGE both in the customer ledger and in the debtors control account.

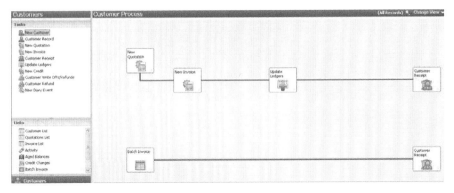

Therefore, if all sales transactions have been entered correctly on SAGE, the total of the balances owed per the sales ledger will always agree with the balance shown per the debtors control account.

As part of your monthly book-keeping routine, it is good practice to make sure that these two totals agree so that any errors can be corrected in a timely manner.

For Prospect Parts, we can see that the balance on the debtors control account as per the trial balance at 31 December 2013 is £1796.27.

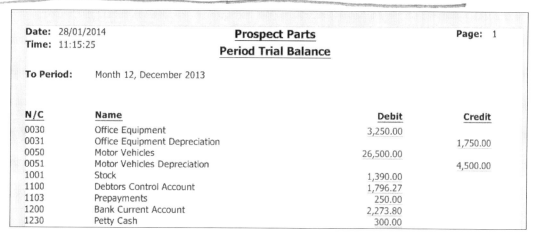

Date: 28/01/2014 Time: 11:15:25	**Prospect Parts** **Period Trial Balance**		Page: 1
To Period: Month 12, December 2013			
N/C **Name**		**Debit**	**Credit**
0030 Office Equipment		3,250.00	
0031 Office Equipment Depreciation			1,750.00
0050 Motor Vehicles		26,500.00	
0051 Motor Vehicles Depreciation			4,500.00
1001 Stock		1,390.00	
1100 Debtors Control Account		1,796.27	
1103 Prepayments		250.00	
1200 Bank Current Account		2,273.80	
1230 Petty Cash		300.00	

We can then check this against the balance shown on the sales ledger at 31 December 2013 by running an aged debtors report at this date:

When running the aged debtors report, take care to make sure the boxes are completed as shown below.

If the aged debtors report is run using a different date to the trial balance from which you have taken the debtors control account balance, or if it is run including future transactions, then this will cause a difference to arise between the two balances due to timing issues.

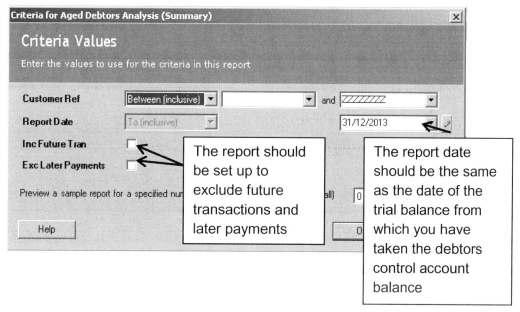

Date: 28/01/2014			**Prospect Parts**						**Page:** 1	
Time: 13:03:38			**Aged Debtors Analysis (Summary)**							

Report Date: 31/12/2013
Include future transactions: No
Exclude later payments: No

Customer From:
Customer To: ZZZZZZZZ

** NOTE: All report values are shown in Base Currency, unless otherwise indicated **

A/C	Name	Credit Limit	Turnover	Balance	Future	Current	Period 1	Period 2	Period 3	Older
GRE001	Green Motors Ltd	£ 1,000.00	526.13	526.13	0.00	0.00	0.00	0.00	0.00	526.13
RED001	Red Motors Ltd	£ 5,000.00	1,022.44	769.88	0.00	769.88	0.00	0.00	0.00	0.00
YEL001	Yellow Motors Ltd	£ 1,500.00	952.36	500.26	0.00	500.26	0.00	0.00	0.00	0.00
	Totals:		2,500.93	1,796.27	0.00	1,270.14	0.00	0.00	0.00	526.13

As can be seen from the aged debtors report above, the sales ledger (list of individual customer balances) agrees with the debtors control account as both show a balance of £1796.27 at 31 December 2013.

3 Identifying errors

Where there is a difference between the total balances per the sales ledger and the balance per the debtors control account, this usually means that a journal has been posted directly to the debtors control account, and so the sales ledger has not been updated at the same time.

To try and prevent such errors from happening, SAGE will flag up any journal entries you make which will cause a difference to arise between your sales ledger and your debtors control account totals.

For example, in the journal shown below, the debtors control account is being credited with £120: because this entry is not being made using the New Credit note function, the sales ledger balances will not be updated for this credit and so a difference will arise:

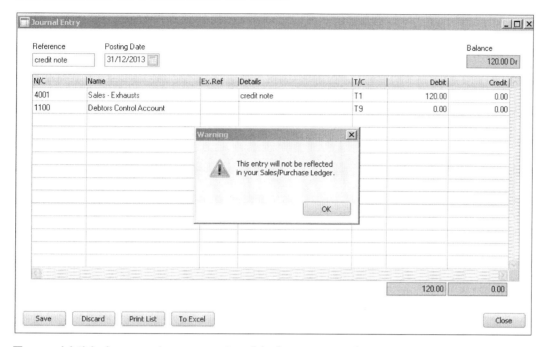

To avoid this happening, you should always use the appropriate option in the Customer Tasks module to enter transactions which need to be reflected in the sales ledger balances.

For illustration purposes only, the journal above has now been posted on SAGE: you should **not** enter this on your SAGE system.

You can see from the reports shown below that the balances shown on the sales ledger and the debtors control account are now different:

Debtor control account:

| Date: 28/01/2014 | Prospect Parts | | Page: 1 |
| Time: 11:45:37 | Period Trial Balance | | |

To Period: Month 12, December 2013

N/C	Name	Debit	Credit
0030	Office Equipment	3,250.00	
0031	Office Equipment Depreciation		1,750.00
0050	Motor Vehicles	26,500.00	
0051	Motor Vehicles Depreciation		4,500.00
1001	Stock	1,390.00	
1100	Debtors Control Account	1,676.27	

Sales Ledger:

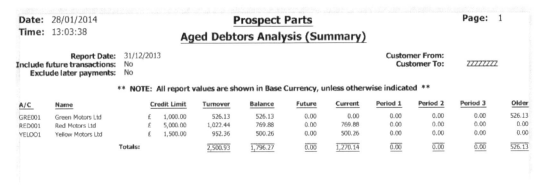

We can use the Maintenance feature on SAGE to help us identify the cause of this difference.

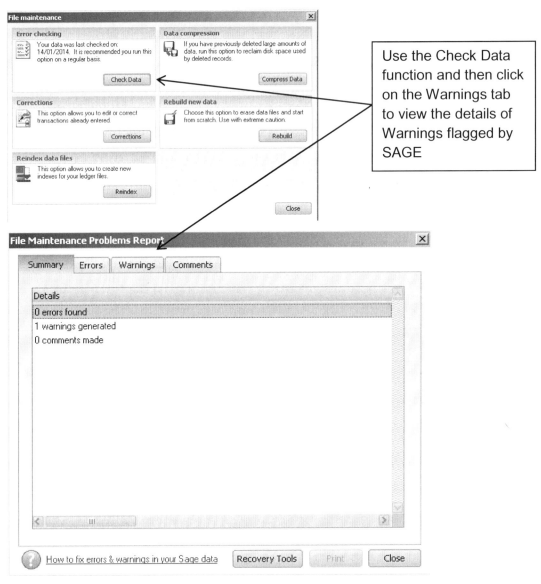

Use the Check Data function and then click on the Warnings tab to view the details of Warnings flagged by SAGE

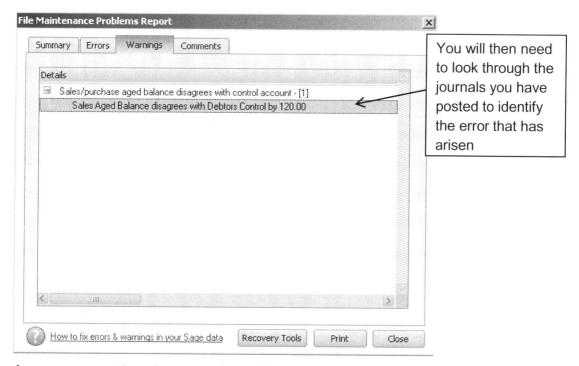

You will then need to look through the journals you have posted to identify the error that has arisen

Any errors can then be amended using a correcting journal to reverse the original incorrect transaction.

4 Reconciling the purchases ledger

The purchases ledger shows the amounts due to individual suppliers at a given date. As with the sales ledger, SAGE allows you to view this information as either a detailed report showing the individual transactions which make up the total supplier balance, or as a summary report which simply shows the total amount owed to each supplier. These reports can be viewed using the Reports function within the Suppliers module.

Purchase invoices, refunds and payments will be entered on SAGE using the Batch Invoice, Supplier Payment, and Supplier Refund functions in the Suppliers module. These transactions will be automatically entered by SAGE both in the purchase ledger and in the creditors control account.

Therefore, if all purchase transactions have been entered correctly on SAGE, the total of the balances owed per the purchase ledger will always agree with the balance shown per the creditors control account.

Again, as part of your monthly book-keeping routine, it is good practice to make sure that these two totals agree so that any errors can be corrected in a timely manner.

The method for reconciling these two balances is exactly the same as the method used for reconciling the sales ledger balance shown in parts two and three of this chapter.

Accruals and prepayments

7

CONTENTS

1 Introduction

Most businesses will need to adjust for accruals and prepayments at the end of their financial period.

An accrual arises where an expense has been incurred in the financial period but has not yet been invoiced or paid and so has not yet been entered on SAGE.

A prepayment arises where an expense relating to a future period has been entered on SAGE as an invoice or a payment in the current financial period.

An adjustment will also be needed for any income which has arisen in the period and has not yet been received, as well as for any income the business has received in advance.

These adjustments ensure that the business applies the accruals concept: in other words, that it recognises all income in the period it is earned rather than in the period it is received and similarly recognises all expenditure in the period it is incurred rather than in the period it is paid.

2 Reversing opening accruals on SAGE

An accrual is an expense which has been incurred during the accounting period, but has not yet been paid or invoiced. This means that it has not yet been entered on SAGE and so the expenses shown in the Profit and Loss Account will not show all the expenses that have arisen during the accounting period.

In order to enter the adjustment for any accruals on SAGE, you will first of all need to reverse any accruals shown in the opening Trial Balance as these relate to expenses incurred in the previous accounting period.

You will enter this adjustment using the Journal Entry screen within the Company Nominal Ledger module.

Looking at Prospect Parts' Trial Balance, you can see that there is an accrual of £200 brought forward in respect of rent. We need to reverse this balance brought forward by posting a journal **debiting** the accruals account N/C2109 with £200 and **crediting** the rent account N/C7100 in the Profit and Loss account with £200.

This journal will have an effect on both the Balance Sheet and the Profit and Loss Account:

- The accruals account N/C2109, shown as a current liability in the Balance Sheet, will be reduced to £nil.

- The rent expense account N/C7100 will be reduced by £200: this is the amount of the rent paid in the current accounting period which actually relates to the previous accounting period.

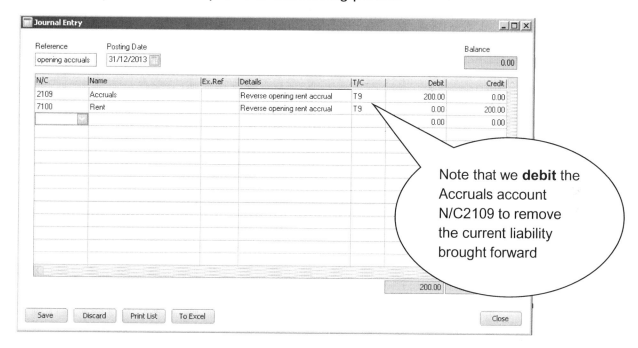

You should check you have entered this journal correctly by reviewing the balances shown on your Nominal Ledger.

- The Accruals account N/C2109, shown as a current liability in the Balance Sheet, now has a balance of £nil

- The Rent account N/C7100, shown as an expense in the Profit and Loss Account, now has a balance of £650: this is the rent expense of £850 as per the opening Trial Balance less the accrual brought forward of £200.

Now you have successfully reversed the opening accrual figure on SAGE, you are ready to post the closing accruals as at 31st December 2013.

3 Entering closing accruals on SAGE

Before you can enter the closing accruals on SAGE, you will need to calculate the amount of any expense that has been incurred but not yet paid at the end of the accounting period.

CASE STUDY

Prospect Parts rents a building at a cost of £100 per month.

During the year ended 31st December 2013 the following payments have been made:

1st January (re November 2012):	£100
1st February (re December 2012):	£100
1st March (re January 2013):	£100
1st April (re February 2013):	£100
1st May (re March 2013):	£100
1st June (re April and May 2013):	£200
1st September (re June and July 2013):	£150

550

Requirement

Calculate the accrual in respect of the rent expense incurred but not paid at 31st December 2013.

Solution

The rent expense incurred but not paid as at 31st December 2013 is as follows:

July (part paid):	£50
August	£100
September	£100
October	£100
November	£100
December	£100
Total rent accrual required	**£550**

You can now enter a journal for this accrual on SAGE using the Journal Entry screen in the Company Nominal Ledger module as before:

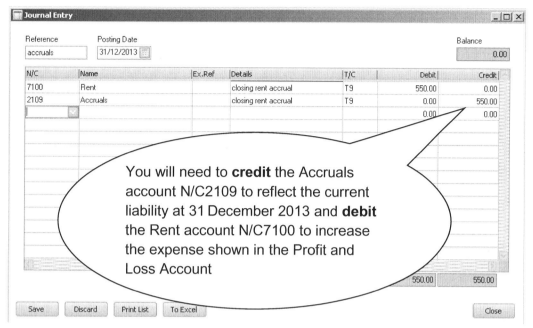

You should check you have entered this journal correctly by reviewing the amounts shown on your Nominal Ledger.

* The Accruals account N/C2109, shown as a current liability in the Balance Sheet, now has a balance of £550.

* The Rent account N/C7100, shown as an expense in the Profit and Loss Account, now shows a balance of £1200: this is the rent expense of £850 as per the opening Trial Balance less the opening accrual of £200 add the closing accrual of £550.

CASE STUDY

Requirement

Prospect Parts Ltd has incurred accountancy fees of £500 in the year.

These have been paid on 31 January 2014.

Input the journal to account for the accrual required on SAGE.

Solution

The journal needs to enter an accrual of £500 in Accruals N/C2109 to be shown as a current liability in the Balance Sheet at 31 December 2013, and an expense of £500 in Accountancy Fees N/C7602 to be shown within the Profit and Loss Account.

Check your journal against the one shown below:

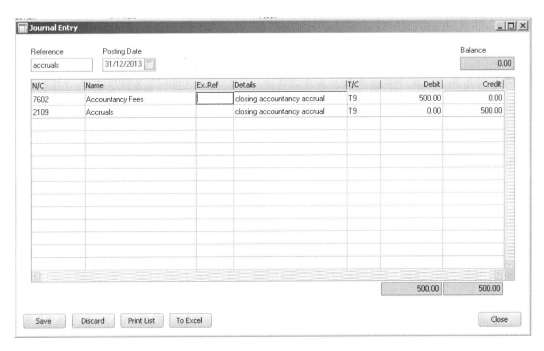

You can now check you have entered this journal correctly by reviewing the balances shown on your Nominal Ledger.

- The Accruals account N/C2109, shown as a current liability in the Balance Sheet, now has a balance of £1050.

  This consists of the rent accrual of £550 and the accountancy fees accrual of £500

- The Accountancy Fees account N/C7100, shown as an expense in the Profit and Loss Account, now shows a balance of £500: this is the accountancy fees expense of £nil as per the opening Trial Balance add the closing accrual of £500.

4 Reversing opening prepayments on SAGE

A prepayment is an expense which has been paid or invoiced during the current accounting period, but which relates to a future period. This means that it has been entered on SAGE and so the Profit and Loss Account will show an expense that relates to a future accounting period.

In order to enter the adjustment for any prepayments on SAGE you will first of all need to reverse any prepayments shown in the opening Trial Balance: these relate to expenses incurred in the current accounting period.

You will enter this adjustment using the Journal Entry screen within the Company Nominal Ledger module.

Looking at Prospect Parts' Trial Balance, you can see that there is a prepayment of £250 brought forward in respect of rates. We need to reverse this balance brought forward, by posting a journal **crediting** the prepayments account N/C1103 with £250 and **debiting** the General Rates account N/C7103 in the Profit and Loss Account with £250.

This journal will have an effect on both the Balance Sheet and the Profit and Loss Account:

*   The Prepayments account N/C1103, shown as a current asset in the Balance Sheet, will be reduced to £nil.

*   The General Rates expense account N/C7103 will be increased by £250: this is the amount of the rates paid in the previous accounting period which actually relates to the current accounting period.

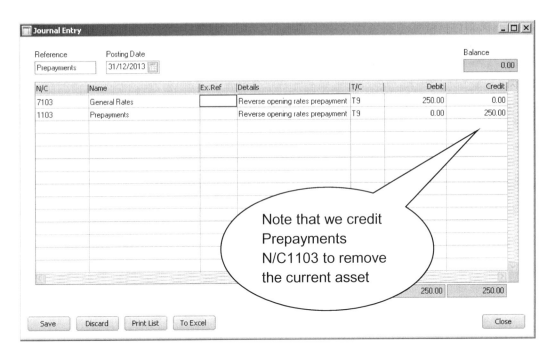

Now check you have entered this journal correctly by reviewing the balances shown on your Nominal Ledger.

*   The Prepayments account N/C1103, shown as a current asset in the Balance Sheet, now has a balance of £nil

*   The General Rates account N/C7103, shown as an expense in the Profit and Loss Account, now has a balance of £1095.62: this is the expense of £845.62 as per the opening Trial Balance add the prepayment brought forward of £250.

Now you have successfully reversed the opening prepayments figure on SAGE, you are ready to post the closing prepayments as at 31st December 2013.

5 Entering closing prepayments on SAGE

As with the accruals above, before you can enter any closing prepayments on SAGE, you will need to calculate the amount of any expense that has been paid in the current accounting period but relates to a future accounting period.

CASE STUDY

On 1 May 2013, Prospect Parts Ltd paid general rates of £800 for the year ending 31st March 2014.

Requirement

Calculate the prepayment in respect of general rates expense as at 31st December 2013.

Solution

The general rates expense paid in the current year which relates to a future accounting period is the part of the payment which covers the months January – March 2014.

This can be calculated as 3/12 × £800 = **£200 prepayment required**

You can now enter a journal for this prepayment on SAGE, using the Journal Entry screen in the Company Nominal Ledger module as before:

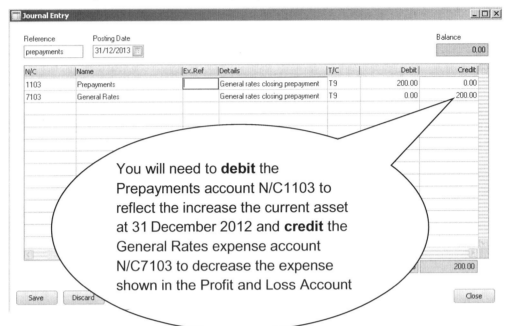

You should now check you have entered this journal correctly by reviewing the amounts shown on your Nominal Ledger.

- The Prepayments account N/C1103, shown as a current asset in the Balance Sheet, now has a balance of £200.

- The General Rates account N/C7103, shown as an expense in the Profit and Loss Account, now shows a balance of £895.62: this is the general rates expense of £845.62 as per the opening Trial Balance add the opening prepayment of £250 less the closing prepayment of £200.

CASE STUDY

Prospect Parts Ltd paid a telephone bill of £75 on 1 December 2013 which relates solely to line rental for the quarter ending 28 February 2014.

Requirement

Calculate the prepayment in respect of telephone expenses as at 31 December 2013 and input the journal to account for this on SAGE.

Solution

The telephone line rental expense paid in the current year which relates to a future accounting period is that part which covers the last two months of the quarter ended 28 February 2014.

This can be calculated as 2/3 × £75 = **£50 prepayment required**

Check your journal against the one shown below:

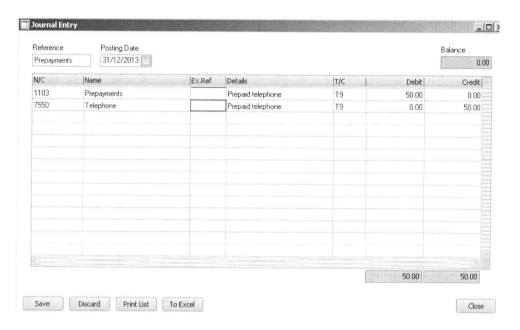

Now check you have entered this journal correctly by reviewing the balances shown on your Nominal Ledger.

- The Prepayments account N/C1103, shown as a current asset in the Balance Sheet, now has a balance of £250.

  This consists of the general rates prepayment of £200 and the telephone prepayment of £50.

- The Telephone account N/C7550, shown as an expense in the Profit and Loss Account, now shows a balance of £559.41: this is the telephone expense of £546.31 as per the opening Trial Balance add the phone bill paid in Chapter 5 of £63.10 less the closing prepayment of £50.

6 Accrued and deferred income

Some businesses have sources of other income which they receive in advance or in arrears which you will also need to adjust for.

Common examples of this include interest receivable and rental income.

Income received in advance of the accounting period in which it is earned is referred to as **Deferred Income**. This income will have been entered on SAGE and so the Profit and Loss Account will show income that relates to a future accounting period.

In order to adjust for deferred income on SAGE, you will need to input a journal which decreases the relevant income account in the Profit and Loss Account, and shows a current liability for deferred income in the Balance Sheet.

Income received after the accounting period in which it is earned is referred to as **Accrued Income**. This income will not have been entered on SAGE and so will not be included as income in the Profit and Loss Account.

In order to adjust for accrued income on SAGE, you will need to post a journal which increases the relevant income account in the Profit and Loss Account, and shows a current asset for accrued income in the Balance Sheet.

CASE STUDY

Prospect Parts Ltd received bank interest of £65 on 31 January 2014 which related to the 6 months ending 31 December 2013.

Requirement

Explain the adjustment required in respect of bank interest receivable as at 31 December 2013 and input the journal to account for this on SAGE.

Solution

The bank interest of £65 received on 31 January 2014 was earned during the year ended 31 December 2013 and so is classified as Accrued Income.

A journal should be prepared which increases Bank Interest Receivable N/C4900, shown as income in the Profit and Loss Account, and increases Accrued Income N/C1101, shown as a current asset in the Balance Sheet.

Note that you will need to rename these two nominal accounts in the default chart of accounts.

Check your journal against the one shown below:

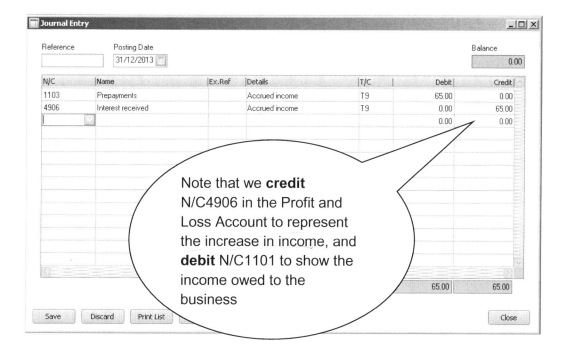

Before moving on to the next chapter, you should check your trial balance on SAGE so far agrees to the one shown below and investigate any differences.

Date: 26/08/2014   **Prospect Parts**   **Page:** 1
Time: 11:04:05   **Period Trial Balance**

To Period: Month 12, December 2013

N/C	Name	Debit	Credit
0030	Office Equipment	3,250.00	
0031	Office Equipment Depreciation		1,750.00
0050	Motor Vehicles	26,500.00	
0051	Motor Vehicles Depreciation		4,500.00
1001	Stock	1,390.00	
1100	Debtors Control Account	1,796.27	
1103	Prepayments	315.00	
1200	Bank Current Account	2,273.80	
1230	Petty Cash	300.00	
2100	Creditors Control Account		3,158.12
2109	Accruals		1,050.00
2201	Purchase Tax Control Account	12.62	
2202	VAT Liability		947.50
3000	Capital		15,715.83
3050	Drawings	5,720.00	
4000	Sales - Tyres		47,224.46
4001	Sales - Exhausts		32,643.27
4002	Sales - Other		9,456.87
4906	Interest received		73.17
5000	Purchases - Tyres	32,534.36	
5001	Purchases - Exhausts	17,668.89	
5002	Purchases - Other	6,879.21	
5200	Opening Stock	900.00	
5201	Closing Stock		1,390.00
7000	Gross Wages	13,520.65	
7100	Rent	1,200.00	
7103	General Rates	895.62	
7304	Miscellaneous Motor Expenses	1,024.36	
7550	Telephone	559.41	
7602	Accountancy Fees	500.00	
7901	Bank Charges	14.60	
8250	Sundry Expenses	654.43	
	Totals:	117,909.22	117,909.22

Provision for bad and doubtful debts

CONTENTS

1 Introduction

When sales are made by a business to a credit customer and the invoice is recorded in SAGE, the double entry created by SAGE is to debit the debtors control account N/C1100 and to credit the sales account N/C4000. This means that the sales income is recognised by the business before the cash has been received, and also a debtor is shown in current assets in respect of the money outstanding.

If the business subsequently has information showing that the debt is unlikely to be paid, or will never be paid, then it should no longer recognise this amount as a current asset, in accordance with the prudence concept. An expense should also be recognised in respect of the bad debt which will reduce the profits for the year.

In order to help identify bad and doubtful debts, the business should regularly use SAGE to produce an Aged Debtors Balances report.

2 Aged debtors balances report

The Aged Debtors Balances report in SAGE allows you to see how much in total each customer owes the business, and how old the debt is. Any balances which are not paid within the business's credit terms will need to be assessed to find out if they are likely to be paid.

To produce the Aged Debtors Balances Report in SAGE you will need to choose the Aged Balances option in the Customers module:

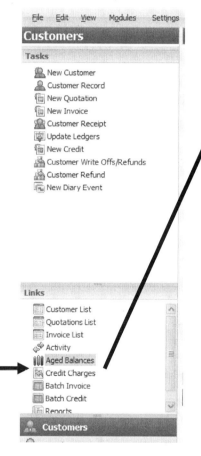

You will then be asked to enter your Aged Balance Report Date: for Prospect Parts Ltd, this is 31 December 2013. You should choose to include payments up to 31 December 2013

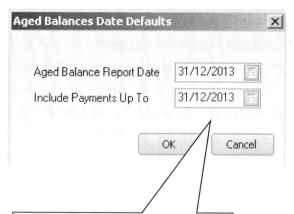

You need to make sure you amend the default date which SAGE will use to include payments from customers. If not, SAGE will automatically choose to include all payments up to today's date.

You should then see the following Aged Debtors Balance report for Prospect Parts Ltd:

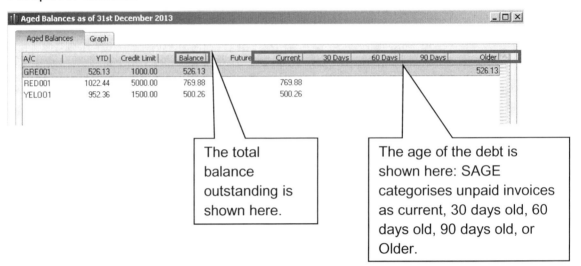

Any old balances appearing on the report should then be investigated: it may be that they are in dispute or the customer has gone out of business, or that an error has been made when posting the customer receipt on SAGE. Any balances which are highly unlikely to be recovered will need to be written off so they are no longer shown as a debtor.

3 Writing off bad debts

When a bad debt is written off, the debtors figure included in current assets on the Balance Sheet will be reduced, and an expense will be shown in the Profit and Loss Account.

The double entry for this is:

DR N/C8100 Bad Debts Write Off

CR N/C1100 Debtors Control Account

To write off a bad debt in SAGE v19, you should use the Customer Write Offs/Refunds wizard which is shown in the Customers module.

Exercise

Look back at chapter 3 in which you posted the customer balances for Prospect Parts Ltd. Dan has told you that he has been in dispute with Green Motors Ltd since February 2013, and so the outstanding balance of £526.13 (including VAT) at 31 December 2013 should be written off as it is not likely to ever be recovered.

Write off this bad debt, using the Customer Write Offs/Refunds wizard.

You will need to follow the steps below:

Select the Customer Write Offs/Refunds option from the Customers module:

You will then need to highlight Write off Customer Transactions and then use the drop down arrow to select the correct customer account:

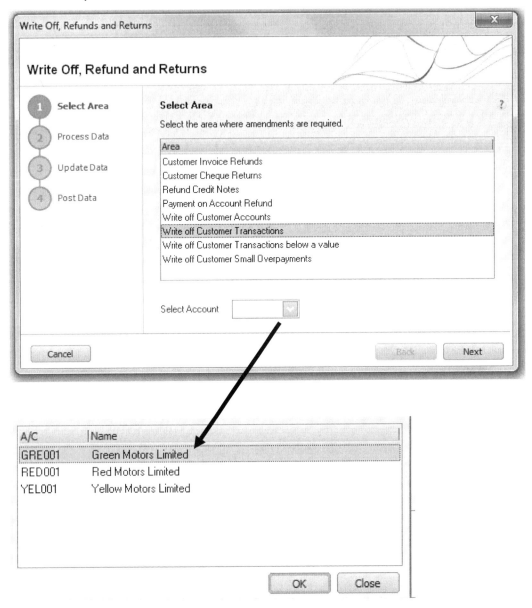

Next, select the correct invoice to be written off:

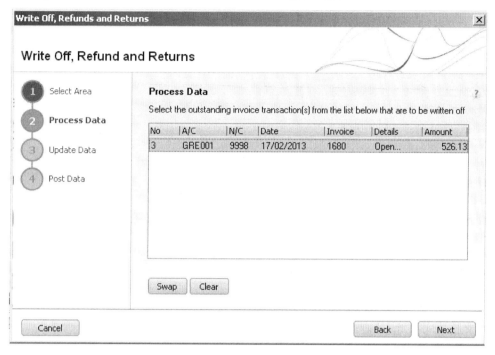

You will then need to check the date of the write off is correct, and add a reference for the write-off:

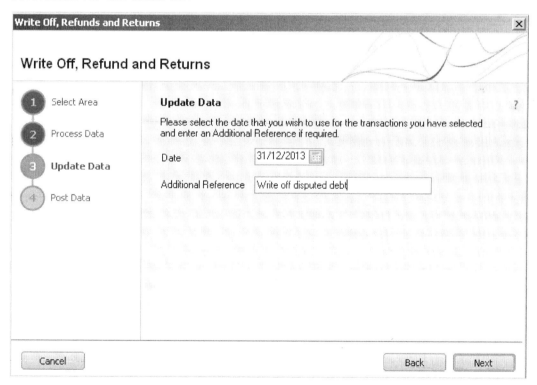

Finally, check that all the information shown is correct, before clicking Post.

You should now check the customer account for Green Motors Ltd to make sure the debt has been written off correctly. This balance now should have been removed from Green Motors Ltd's account.

The bad debt write off will affect both the Balance Sheet and the Profit and Loss Account.

The Debtors Control account N/C1100 shown in current assets will be reduced (as we have credited it with the bad debt written off).

There will also be a debit balance in the Bad Debt Write Off account N/C8100 of £526.13 which is an expense and so reduces the profits shown in the Profit and Loss Account.

4 VAT and bad debt relief

If a business is VAT registered, it will generally charge customers VAT on goods and services sold on credit. If the customer subsequently does not pay for these items, the business can claim that VAT back which it has paid to HMRC but not received from the customer. This is known as Bad Debt Relief.

The following criteria must be met:

- The debt is at least six months old and less than four years and six months old
- The debt has been written off in the accounts
- The debt has not been sold or handed on to a factoring company

For more information, please see the HMRC website: www.hmrc.gov.uk

On SAGE, you will need to enter the VAT that can be claimed back using a journal entry.

Exercise

Dan tells you that the bad debt written off above re Green Motors Ltd meets all of HMRC's criteria for bad debt relief.

Prepare the journal entry on SAGE to obtain the bad debt relief following the steps below:

First of all, calculate the amount of bad debt relief that can be obtained. The balance written off is £526.13. This includes VAT at 20%, and so the VAT element will be: 20/120 × £526.13 = £87.68.

Next, choose the Journal Entry option from the Company module:

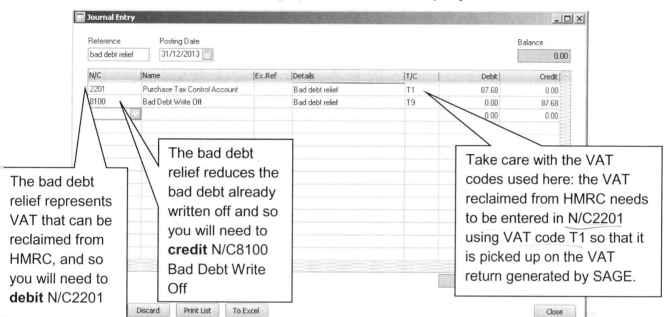

Click Save to complete the transaction.

After completing these transactions, your trial balance should look like this:

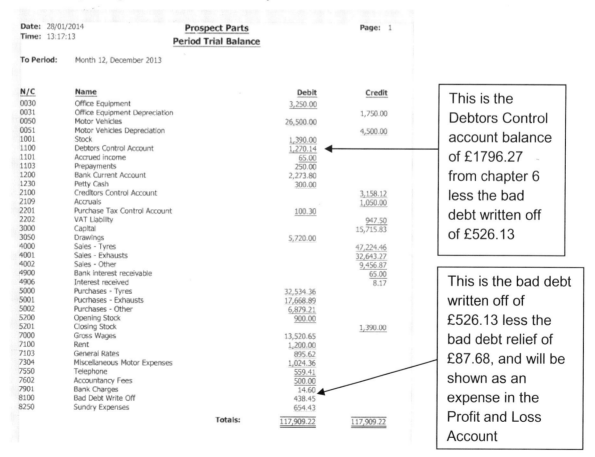

5 Provision for doubtful debts

In the previous section, we looked at how to deal with debts which were certain not to be recovered and so needed writing off.

Sometimes, the business may not be certain that a debt will not be recovered but may have doubts about this. This is known as a doubtful debt.

To deal with doubtful debts, we debit N/C8102 Bad Debt Provision account, which is shown in the Profit and Loss Account, and credit N/C1106 Provision for Doubtful Debts in SAGE: this account is then netted off by SAGE in the Balance Sheet against the Debtors Control Account to reduce current assets.

There are two types of provisions for doubtful debts that can be made by a business, both are which are accounted for in the same way in SAGE.

Specific Provision: this is made in respect of specific debts which the business feels may not be paid: e.g. debts older than 90 days.

General Provision: This is made in respect of trade debtors as a whole, and expressed as a percentage: e.g. a business may find from experience that 2% of debts will not be paid. This percentage should be applied to the total trade debtors figure, after any specific bad debts have been written off, and after any specific provisions for doubtful debts have been made.

Exercise

Dan believes that 3% of the total trade debtors balances may not be paid.

Prepare the journal entry on SAGE to account for this general doubtful debts provision.

Remember: you will need to base the provision on the total trade debtors figure shown in the trial balance **after** writing off the bad debt due from Green Motors Ltd in the exercise above.

The first step is to calculate the general doubtful debts provision required.

The debtors control account shows a balance of £1270.14, after writing off the bad debt re Green Motors Ltd. Prospect Parts Ltd needs a general provision of 3% of this, which gives £38.10.

This is then entered on SAGE using a journal entry:

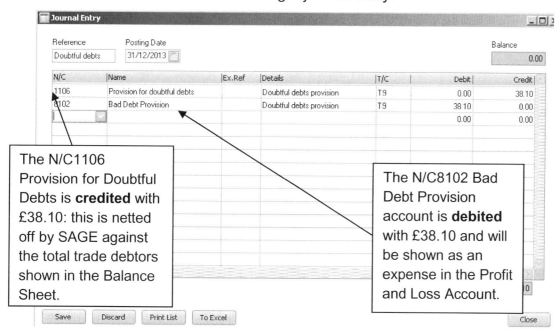

The N/C1106 Provision for Doubtful Debts is **credited** with £38.10: this is netted off by SAGE against the total trade debtors shown in the Balance Sheet.

The N/C8102 Bad Debt Provision account is **debited** with £38.10 and will be shown as an expense in the Profit and Loss Account.

Click Save to complete the journal entry.

Note that this journal does not affect the individual customer balances in any way and your N/C1100 debtors control account will still show a total balance of £1270.14.

Changes in the Provision for Doubtful Debts

As the N/C1106 Provision for Doubtful Debts account is a Balance Sheet account, this balance will be shown in the Balance Sheet until it is changed by another journal entry.

When the provision needs to be updated in the future, you will therefore only need to enter the total increase or decrease on SAGE.

If the Provision for Doubtful Debts needs to be **increased** in the future, you will need to enter the increase on SAGE as follows:

> DR N/C8102 Bad Debt Provision – to reflect the additional expense in the Profit and Loss Account

> CR N/C1106 Provision of Doubtful Debts – to reflect the increase in the provision in the Balance Sheet.

If the Provision for Doubtful Debts needs to be **reduced** in the future, the decrease should be entered on SAGE as:

> DR N/C1106 – to reflect the decrease in the overall provision in the Balance Sheet

> CR N/C8102 – to reflect the decrease in the provision in the Profit and Loss Account

You should now check that your trial balance agrees with the one shown below to make sure you have entered all of these adjustments correctly, and investigate any differences in your answer.

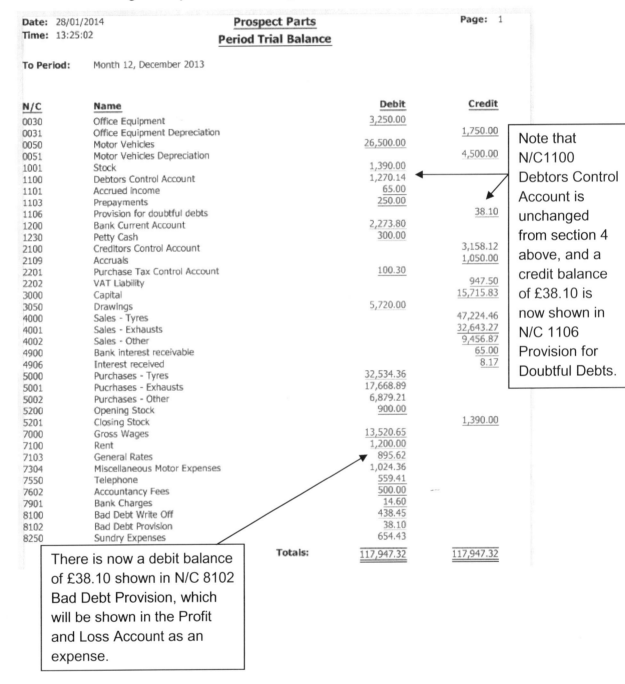

| Date: 28/01/2014 | Prospect Parts | Page: 1 | |
| Time: 13:25:02 | Period Trial Balance | | |

To Period: Month 12, December 2013

N/C	Name	Debit	Credit
0030	Office Equipment	3,250.00	
0031	Office Equipment Depreciation		1,750.00
0050	Motor Vehicles	26,500.00	
0051	Motor Vehicles Depreciation		4,500.00
1001	Stock	1,390.00	
1100	Debtors Control Account	1,270.14	
1101	Accrued income	65.00	
1103	Prepayments	250.00	
1106	Provision for doubtful debts		38.10
1200	Bank Current Account	2,273.80	
1230	Petty Cash	300.00	
2100	Creditors Control Account		3,158.12
2109	Accruals		1,050.00
2201	Purchase Tax Control Account	100.30	
2202	VAT Liability		947.50
3000	Capital		15,715.83
3050	Drawings	5,720.00	
4000	Sales - Tyres		47,224.46
4001	Sales - Exhausts		32,643.27
4002	Sales - Other		9,456.87
4900	Bank interest receivable		65.00
4906	Interest received		8.17
5000	Purchases - Tyres	32,534.36	
5001	Pucrhases - Exhausts	17,668.89	
5002	Purchases - Other	6,879.21	
5200	Opening Stock	900.00	
5201	Closing Stock		1,390.00
7000	Gross Wages	13,520.65	
7100	Rent	1,200.00	
7103	General Rates	895.62	
7304	Miscellaneous Motor Expenses	1,024.36	
7550	Telephone	559.41	
7602	Accountancy Fees	500.00	
7901	Bank Charges	14.60	
8100	Bad Debt Write Off	438.45	
8102	Bad Debt Provision	38.10	
8250	Sundry Expenses	654.43	
	Totals:	117,947.32	117,947.32

Note that N/C1100 Debtors Control Account is unchanged from section 4 above, and a credit balance of £38.10 is now shown in N/C 1106 Provision for Doubtful Debts.

There is now a debit balance of £38.10 shown in N/C 8102 Bad Debt Provision, which will be shown in the Profit and Loss Account as an expense.

The extracts below show you how the bad debt provision and the bad debts expense will appear in the Balance Sheet and the Profit and Loss Account.

Extract from the Balance Sheet

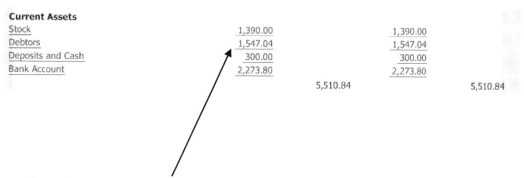

Current Assets		
Stock	1,390.00	1,390.00
Debtors	1,547.04	1,547.04
Deposits and Cash	300.00	300.00
Bank Account	2,273.80	2,273.80
	5,510.84	5,510.84

Note that the total debtors figure consists of the following balances:

Date:	28/01/2014	**Prospect Parts**	Page: 1
Time:	13:27:27	**Category Breakdown Period (Balance Sheet)**	

From:	Month 1, January 2013
To:	Month 12, December 2013

Chart of Accounts: Default Layout of Accounts

			Period	Year to Date
Current Assets				
Debtors				
1100	Debtors Control Account		1,270.14	1,270.14
1101	Accrued income		65.00	65.00
1103	Prepayments		250.00	250.00
1106	Provision for doubtful debts		(38.10)	(38.10)
			1,547.04	1,547.04

Extract from the Profit and Loss Account

Overheads

Gross Wages	13,520.65	13,520.65
Rent and Rates	2,095.62	2,095.62
Motor Expenses	1,024.36	1,024.36
Telephone and Computer charges	559.41	559.41
Professional Fees	500.00	500.00
Bank Charges and Interest	14.60	14.60
Bad Debts	476.55	476.55
General Expenses	654.43	654.43
	18,845.62	18,845.62

The Bad Debts expense shown in the Profit and Loss Account is made up as follows:

Date: 28/01/2014   **Prospect Parts**   **Page:** 1
Time: 13:29:33   **Category Breakdown (Profit and Loss)**

From: Month 1, January 2013
To: Month 12, December 2013

Chart of Accounts: Default Layout of Accounts

		Period	Year to Date
Overheads			
Bad Debts			
8100	Bad Debt Write Off	438.45	438.45
8102	Bad Debt Provision	38.10	38.10
		476.55	476.55

Fixed assets

9

CONTENTS

1 Introduction
2 Fixed asset categories
3 Acquisitions of tangible fixed assets
4 Disposals of tangible fixed assets
5 Depreciation
6 Revaluations
7 Intangible fixed assets

1 Introduction

A fixed asset is an asset which is held for continuing use in a business for the generation of profits, and is not purchased for resale.

There are two types of fixed assets which can be held by a business:

Tangible fixed assets are assets which can be physically touched, such as a car, building or machine.

Intangible fixed assets are assets which cannot be physically touched but which are controlled by the business and are intended to be used to generate future profits, such as goodwill.

Expenditure which can be capitalised as an asset is referred to as **capital expenditure**. Expenditure which is shown in the Profit and Loss Account is known as **revenue expenditure**.

2 Fixed asset categories

SAGE v19 has six tangible fixed assets categories already set up in the default chart of accounts:

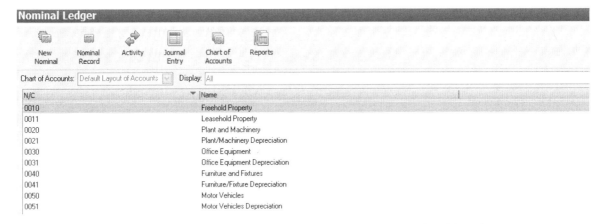

You can also add new categories at any time, as required by the business, using the New Nominal button shown in the Nominal Ledger option within the Company module: see chapter 2 for more detail.

Note that you will need to create a new nominal account code for any intangible assets held by the business.

приобретание

3 Acquisitions of tangible fixed assets

All tangible fixed assets must be initially recognised at cost: this is the purchase price of an asset (after deducting any trade discounts or rebates), as well as any other costs directly attributable to bringing the asset into working condition for its intended use.

Directly attributable costs as set out in current UK accounting standards include:

- Labour costs of the business's employees arising from the construction or acquisition of the fixed asset.

- Any incremental costs incurred by the business in the course of acquiring the asset, which would not otherwise have arisen.

Examples of such directly attributable costs include: site preparation costs, delivery costs, acquisition costs and installation fees.

The cost of an asset will, however, exclude any administration and general overhead costs, as well as any abnormal costs such as those relating to design errors, industrial disputes and other production delays.

Example

A business purchases a new machine for its workshop. The following costs are incurred:

	£
Purchase price	20,000 ✓
Delivery costs	1,500 ✓
Specialist installation fee	2,000 ✓
Trade discount received	– (600)
Repair of design fault	2,500 ✓
	25,400

Requirement

What is the initial cost of the machine to be recorded as a fixed asset?

Solution

The repair of the design fault is classed as an abnormal cost and so cannot be included as part of the initial capital cost of the machine. Instead, this will be shown as an expense in the Profit and Loss Account.

	Total	Capitalise	Charge to P&L
	£	£	£
Purchase price	20,000	20,000	
Delivery costs	1,500	1,500	
Specialist installation fee	2,000	2,000	
Trade discount received	(600)	(600)	
Repair of design fault	2,500		2,500
	25,400	**22,900**	**2,500**

When you record the purchase of a tangible fixed asset, you will need to take care that you allocate the cost to the correct code in SAGE: the depreciation codes N/C0021, N/C0031, N/C0041 and N/C0051 should **not** be used to record the cost. These codes are only used to record the depreciation of assets, covered later in this chapter.

Exercise

Prospect Parts purchased a machine for £600 (including VAT) on 31st December 2013. This was paid for by cheque no 27 from the company bank account.

Record the purchase of the new machine on SAGE.

Step one: You will need to select the Bank Payments option within the Bank module.

Step two: You will then need to enter the purchase details as shown below:

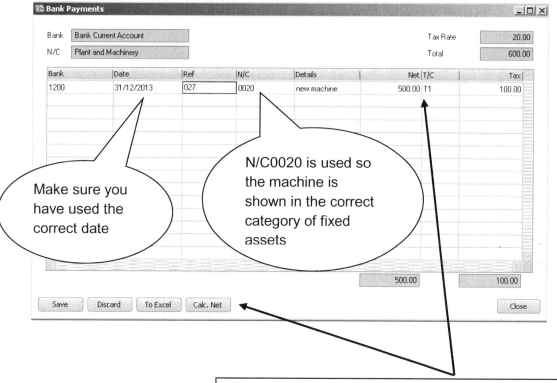

Finally, click Save to enter the transaction on SAGE.

You will now be able to see this new balance shown on the nominal ledger:

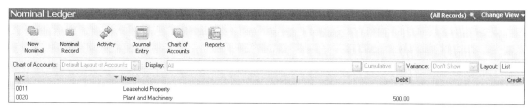

4 Disposals of tangible fixed assets

When a tangible fixed asset is sold or scrapped, we need to remove the cost and accumulated depreciation for that asset from the fixed asset totals shown in the Balance Sheet. This ensures that our Balance Sheet does not include any fixed assets which the business no longer owns. We then match these with the proceeds received on the sale of the asset, using N/C4200 Sale of Assets in SAGE v19: the balancing figure on this account is our profit or loss on disposal.

Exercise

Dan tells you that Prospect Parts sold one of its vans for £6,000 (including VAT) on 31 December 2013.

This van had an original cost of £10,000 and there is accumulated depreciation of £4,000 in respect of this vehicle.

Requirement

Account for this disposal in SAGE.

Step one: Use a journal entry to remove the cost of the van from N/C0050 Motor Vehicles, and transfer it to N/C4200 Sale of Assets. This will ensure that the cost of the van is no longer shown as part of the fixed assets total in the Balance Sheet.

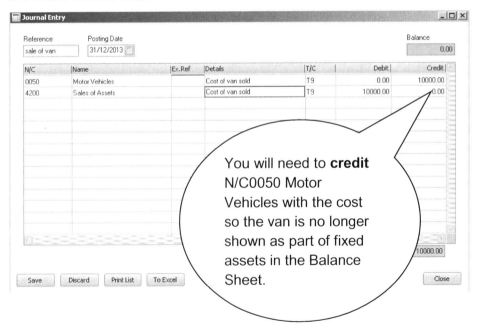

Step two: Use a journal entry to remove the accumulated depreciation in respect of this van: this will ensure that the total accumulated depreciation shown in the Balance Sheet only relates to fixed assets still held by the company at 31 December 2013.

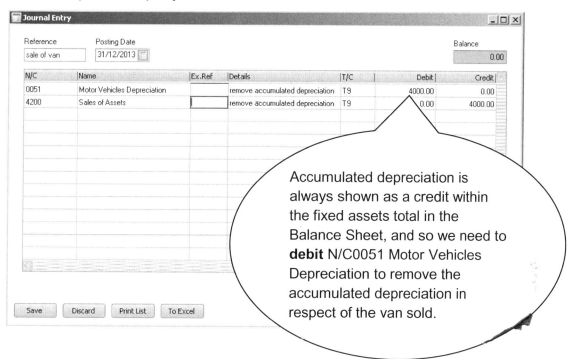

Accumulated depreciation is always shown as a credit within the fixed assets total in the Balance Sheet, and so we need to **debit** N/C0051 Motor Vehicles Depreciation to remove the accumulated depreciation in respect of the van sold.

Step three: Enter the sales proceeds using the Bank Receipts button within the Bank module:

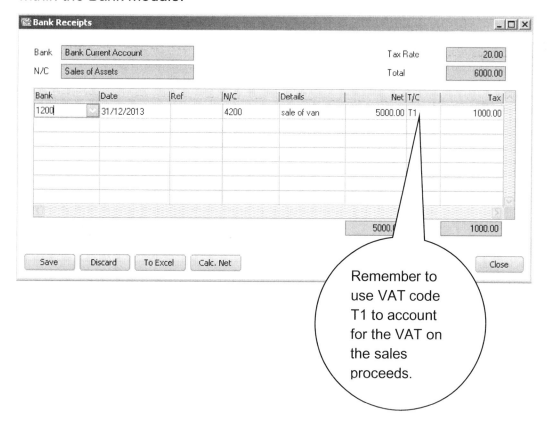

Remember to use VAT code T1 to account for the VAT on the sales proceeds.

Step four: check the nominal ledger on SAGE to make sure that all balances have been correctly updated.

N/C0050 Motor Vehicles had an opening balance of £26,500: this has been reduced by £10,000 to remove the cost of the van sold, and now shows a balance of £16,500.

N/C0051 Motor Vehicles Depreciation had an opening balance of £4,500: this has been reduced by £4,000 to remove the accumulated depreciation in respect of the van sold, and now shows a balance of £500.

N/C4200 Sales of Assets shows the difference between the net book value of the van of £10,000 – £4,000 = £6,000, and the sales proceeds (excluding VAT) of £5,000. The sales proceeds are less than the net book value of the van at the disposal date, and so there is a loss on disposal of £1,000. This will be shown as an expense in the Profit and Loss Account, and so is a debit balance.

Exercise

Dan also tells you that Prospect Parts sold a photocopier, currently included in Office Equipment, for £120 (including VAT) on 31 December 2013.

This photocopier is included in Office Equipment at a cost of £600, and was purchased on 1 June 2010.

The company's depreciation policy in respect of Office Equipment is to charge deprecation on a straight line basis at a rate of 20% per annum, charging a full year's depreciation in the year of acquisition and none in the year of disposal.

Requirement

Account for this disposal in SAGE.

Step One: Remove the cost of the photocopier from N/C0030 so that the photocopier is no longer included within the fixed assets total in the Balance Sheet.

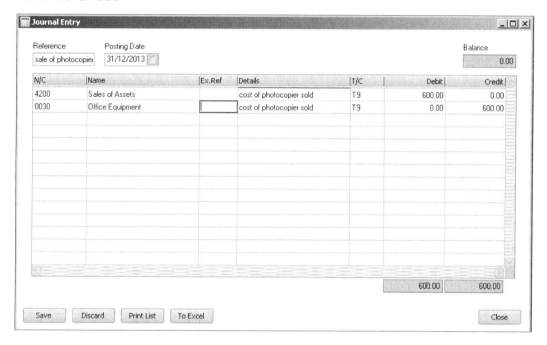

Step two: Remove the accumulated depreciation in respect of the photocopier so it is no longer shown in the Balance Sheet.

You are not given this information, so will need to perform a separate working here.

Depreciation is charged at a rate of 20% per annum on a straight line basis, and so the annual deprecation charge is £600 × 20% = £120.

A full year's charge is made in the year of acquisition, and none in the year of disposal, so depreciation will have been charged for three years (2010, 2011 and 2012).

The accumulated depreciation in respect of this photocopier is therefore 3 × £120 = £360.

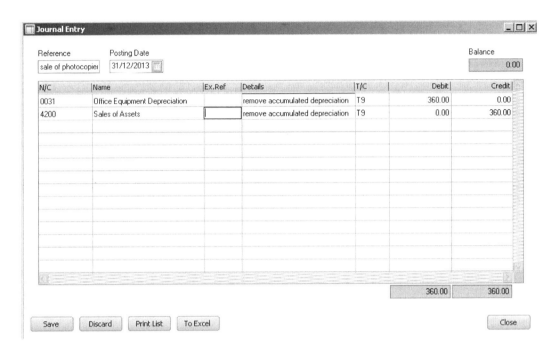

Step three: Enter the sales proceeds using the Bank Receipts button within the Bank module:

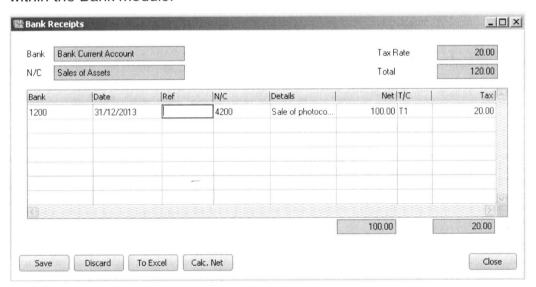

Step four: check the nominal ledger on SAGE to make sure that all balances have been correctly updated.

N/C0030 Office Equipment had an opening balance of £3,250: this has been reduced by £600 to remove the cost of the photocopier sold, and now shows a balance of £2,650.

N/C0031 Office Equipment Depreciation had an opening balance of £1,750: this has been reduced by £360 to remove the accumulated depreciation in respect of the photocopier sold, and now shows a balance of £1,390.

N/C4200 Sales of Assets shows the difference between the net book value of the photocopier of £600 – £360 = £240, and the sales proceeds (excluding VAT) of £100. The sales proceeds are less than the net book value of the photocopier at the disposal date, and so there is a loss on disposal of £140. This will be shown as an expense in the Profit and Loss Account, and so is a debit balance.

The activity in N/C4200 is shown below so you can clearly see how the total loss on disposal of £1,140 has arisen.

The account balance is £1,140 debit, so this will be shown as an expense in the Profit and Loss Account: £1,000 relates to the loss on the disposal of the van shown in the first example above, and £140 relates to the loss on the disposal of the photocopier in the second example above.

N/C:	4200		Name:	Sales of Assets				Account Balance:		1,140.00 DR		
No	**Type**	**Date**	**Account**	**Ref**	**Details**	**Dept**	**T/C**	**Value**	**Debit**	**Credit**	**V**	**B**
100	JD	31/12/2013	4200	sale of van	Cost of van sold	0	T9	10,000.00	10,000.00		-	-
102	JC	31/12/2013	4200	sale of van	remove accumulated	0	T9	4,000.00		4,000.00	-	-
103	BR	31/12/2013	1200		sale of van	0	T1	5,000.00		5,000.00	N	N
104	JD	31/12/2013	4200	sale of	cost of photocopier sold	0	T9	600.00	600.00		-	-
107	JC	31/12/2013	4200	sale of	remove accumulated	0	T9	360.00		360.00	-	-
108	BR	31/12/2013	1200		Sale of photocopier	0	T1	100.00		100.00	N	N
							Totals:		10,600.00	9,460.00		
							History Balance:		1,140.00			

5 Depreciation

Depreciation is the measure of the cost of the economic benefits of a fixed asset consumed by the business during the accounting period. It matches the cost of the asset to the benefits that asset generates.

All fixed assets, other than freehold land, have a finite life and so should be depreciated.

The depreciable amount of a fixed asset (the cost less any residual value) should be written off over the useful economic life of the asset (the period over which the business expects to derive an economic benefit from the asset).

For the Level III Syllabus, you need to know how to enter depreciation on SAGE using both the straight line and the reducing balance methods. These are both covered in detail in Level III Manual study text, but a brief example of each method has been provided below as a reminder.

Example

A machine costs £2,000. Its estimated useful life is four years. It is expected to have a residual scrap value of £100.

Requirement: Calculate the depreciation charge for each of the four years using:

(i) The straight line basis

(ii) The reducing balance basis at a rate of 25%.

Solution

(i)   The depreciation charge on a straight line basis for each of the four years will be calculated as: (£2,000 – £100)/4 = £475

(ii) The depreciation charge on a reducing balance basis at a rate of 25% for each of the four years will be:

	Depreciation charge £	NBV £
Year 1: £2,000 × 25%	500	1,500
Year 2: £1,500 × 25%	375	1,125
Year 3: £1,125 × 25%	281	844
Year 4: £844 × 25%	211	633

Entering Depreciation on SAGE

Before you can enter the depreciation charge for the year on SAGE, you will need to deal with any additions and disposals of tangible fixed assets that have occurred during the year. You can then calculate the depreciation charge for the year in respect of all classes of fixed assets and enter this on SAGE.

You have already dealt with all of the fixed asset additions and disposals for Prospect Parts for the year ended 31 December 2013.

Before proceeding any further, you should check that your nominal ledger balances for the fixed asset accounts agree with the balances shown below:

N/C	Name	Debit	Credit
0010	Freehold Property		
0011	Leasehold Property		
0020	Plant and Machinery	500.00	
0021	Plant/Machinery Depreciation		
0030	Office Equipment	2650.00	
0031	Office Equipment Depreciation		1390.00
0040	Furniture and Fixtures		
0041	Furniture/Fixture Depreciation		
0050	Motor Vehicles	16500.00	
0051	Motor Vehicles Depreciation		500.00

Now you need to use the information below to calculate the depreciation charge for the year.

Exercise

Prospect Parts depreciates its tangible fixed assets on the following bases:

  Motor Vehicles – 25% per annum on a reducing balance basis

  Plant and Machinery – 25% per annum on a straight line basis

  Office Equipment – 20% per annum on a straight line basis

A full year's depreciation is charged in the year of acquisition and none in the year of disposal.

Requirement: calculate the depreciation charge for each class of fixed assets for the year and enter this on SAGE.

Step one: Using the balances shown on the nominal ledger, calculate the depreciation charge for each class of asset.

Note that the balances shown on the nominal ledger have already been adjusted for fixed assets purchased and sold during the year, and so you will be basing your depreciation calculations on the correct cost and net book value of assets.

Motor Vehicles: N/C0050 Motor Vehicles shows a total cost of £16,500, and N/C0051 shows a total accumulated depreciation of £500, giving a net book value of £16,000 for motor vehicles.

The depreciation charge for the year for motor vehicles will be 25% × £16,000 = £4,000.

Plant and Machinery: N/C0020 Plant and Machinery shows a total cost of £500.

The depreciation charge for the year for plant and machinery will be £500 × 25% = £125.

Office Equipment: N/C0030 Office Equipment shows a total cost of £2,650.

The depreciation charge for the year in respect of office equipment will be £2,650 × 20% = £530

Step two: Enter the depreciation journal on SAGE. This can be entered either as one journal, or three separate journals, one for each class of asset.

Remember that the depreciation charge for the year affects both the Profit and Loss account and the Balance Sheet.

We will **debit** the relevant depreciation expense accounts N/C8000 – N/C8004 with the depreciation charge for the year. This will be shown as the total depreciation expense in the Profit and Loss Account for the year.

We will **credit** the relevant depreciation accounts N/C0021, N/C0031, N/C0041 and/or N/C0051 with the depreciation charge for the year. These are Balance Sheet accounts and so show the cumulative depreciation charged to date for each class of assets. These depreciation accounts will reduce the cost of the fixed assets shown in the Balance Sheet.

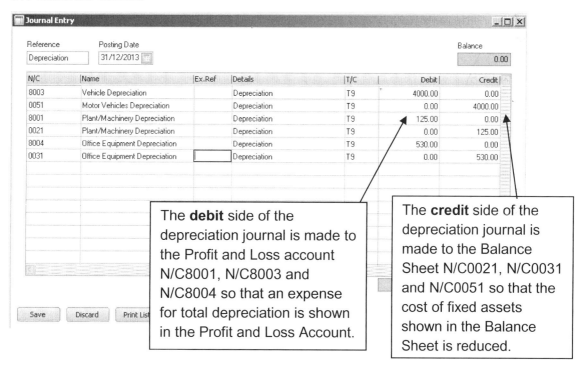

We can now look in the Company module, in the Financials tab, to see how these balances are shown in the accounts.

In the extract from the Profit and Loss Account below, we can see that there is a total depreciation expense for the year of £4,655.

Overheads

Gross Wages	13,520.65	13,520.65
Rent and Rates	2,095.62	2,095.62
Motor Expenses	1,024.36	1,024.36
Telephone and Computer charges	559.41	559.41
Professional Fees	500.00	500.00
Bank Charges and Interest	14.60	14.60
Depreciation	4,655.00	4,655.00

The extract from the Balance Sheet below shows the net book value (i.e. cost less accumulated depreciation) of each class of fixed asset at the end of the financial year:

Fixed Assets

Plant and Machinery	375.00		375.00	
Office Equipment	730.00		730.00	
Motor Vehicles	12,000.00		12,000.00	
		13,105.00		13,105.00

This is made up as follows:

	Cost £	Accumulated Depreciation £	Net Book Value £
Plant and Machinery	500	125	375
Office Equipment	2650	1920	730
Motor Vehicles	16500	4500	12000
Totals	**19650**	**6545**	**13105**

6 Revaluations

Any gains on revaluation will be credited to the revaluation reserve in SAGE. A nominal code in the range of 3100 – 3299 should be used for this.

The balance on the revaluation reserve, along with the trading profit or loss for the year, will be transferred to the proprietor's capital account at the end of the year.

Example

A building costing £100,000 was purchased on 1st January 2012.

On 31st December 2013, the building was revalued to £120,000.

Show how this revaluation would be entered on SAGE for the year ended 31st December 2013.

Solution

The cost of the property will need to be increased to its revalued amount, so we will need to **debit** £20,000 to N/C0010 Freehold Property.

The revaluation gain is the difference between the revalued carrying value and the current carrying value, which is £120,000 – £100,000 = £20,000.

We will need to **Credit** this to N/C3102 Revaluation reserve to show this as a reserve in the Balance Sheet which will be transferred to the proprietor's capital account at the year end.

The journal to enter on SAGE will be:

DR N/C0010 Freehold property   £20,000

CR N/C3102 Revaluation Reserve   £20,000

7 Intangible fixed assets

Intangible fixed assets are assets without physical substance and include goodwill, patents, licences and development costs.

Intangible fixed assets are capitalised at cost: you will need to create a new nominal code in SAGE for any intangible fixed assets held by the business.

You will also need to calculate an amortisation charge for each intangible asset: again, a new nominal code in SAGE will need to be set up for this. Amortisation is calculated over the life of the asset, in the same way as depreciation is for a tangible fixed asset. In the case of goodwill, current UK accounting standards set out that goodwill should usually be amortised over a period not exceeding 20 years.

As with tangible fixed assets above, SAGE will then show the amortisation charge for the year in the Profit and Loss Account, and the net book value of the asset, so cost less accumulated amortisation, in the Balance Sheet.

VAT returns

CONTENTS

1 Introduction

Businesses must register for VAT if their turnover in any twelve month period is, or is expected to be, above a certain level. In 2014-15 this is £81,000. Businesses may also elect to register voluntarily.

Once registered a business must submit a VAT Return on a quarterly basis to HM Revenue and Customs. This can be in paper format or electronically – although HMRC expect most businesses to submit their return online. With this return the relevant VAT payment must be submitted (occasionally a VAT rebate may be claimed).

There are significant penalties for any business failing to meet its obligations under VAT registration, and so it is important that businesses account correctly and promptly for their VAT liabilities.

VAT is charged at different rates:

Standard Rated	20%
Lower Rated	5% (Certain goods and services such as domestic fuel)
Zero Rated	0% (Including most foods, books, newspapers and children's clothes)

Further details on VAT are available from www.hmrc.gov.uk

Some goods and services also fall outside the scope of VAT and are therefore exempt.

The liability to VAT is calculated by:

VAT charged on sales that the business has made *(Output Tax)*

Minus

VAT paid on purchases that the business has made *(Input Tax)*

2   Manual reconciliation of VAT liability

SAGE will calculate the VAT liability quickly and easily, but you should always check the figures as there are likely to be significant implications for the business if incorrect information is submitted to HM Revenue and Customs.

To allow you to see where the figures on the VAT Return produced by SAGE originate from, consider again all the transactions you have entered so far. Some of these will have VAT implications, and others will not.

Firstly, preview (and if you wish print) a **Detailed Audit Trail** (from the

Company – Financials module – press the Audit Trail button) for the period 01/01/2013 to 31/12/2013. This will show you a breakdown of every single transaction that you have entered during this period.

It should look like this:

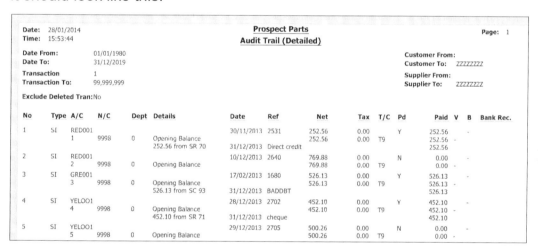

There should be approximately eight pages in total.

This details, in entry order, every transaction entered, starting with the very first entry you made which was the Opening Balance (£252.56) for Red Motors Ltd, right up to the last transaction (Depreciation).

This report also breaks down the VAT element of any transaction.

Working through the list you should now find and identify the following:

VAT on sales

No	Type	Details		Net	Tax
103	SR	Sale of van		5000.00	1000.00
108	SR	Sale of photocopier		100.00	20.00
			Total	**5100.00**	**1020.00**

Note: The numbers in the 'No' column may be slightly different in your report if, for example, you have had to make a correction to an entry. You should still be able to identify the entries above.

The **Type** in the audit trail helps you to identify what type of transaction you entered. Here:

SI = Sales Invoice

SR = Sales Receipt

These result in an increase in the VAT liability for the business, as it has collected VAT from the customer.

However:

SC = Sales Credit.

A sales credit entry will represent a reduction in the VAT liability.

So the total **Output Tax** for the quarter is £1020.00

Now identify the following purchase transactions from the Audit Trail:

VAT on purchases

No	Type	Details	Net	Tax
73	BP	Tiny Telecom	63.10	12.62 ✓
98	BP	New Machine	500.00	100.00 √
94	JD	Bad debt relief	87.68	87.68
		Total	650.78	200.30

Here, the following Types of transaction are listed:

PI   Purchase Invoice

BP   Bank Payment

CP   Cash Payment

JD   Journal Debit

These all have elements of VAT which the business has paid and can now reclaim. Note that the Journal Debit will arise where bad debt relief is being claimed by the business.

However, there is also:

PC   Purchase Credit

A Purchase Credit will be created because of a purchase return which will reduce the amount of VAT the business can reclaim against its liability

So the total **Input Tax** is £200.30

3 Using SAGE to produce the VAT return

From the **COMPANY – FINANCIALS** module, click on the %o VAT Return button. This will bring up a window which represents the VAT100 quarterly VAT Return. Enter the correct dates for the return (in this case 1st October 2013 – 31st December 2013) and click the Calculate button.

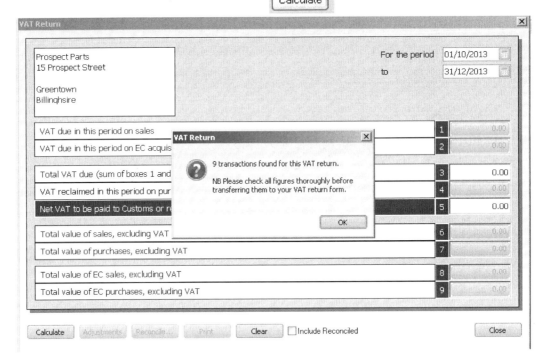

SAGE now indicates how many transactions there are within this particular VAT period and advises you to check the figures thoroughly. Click OK

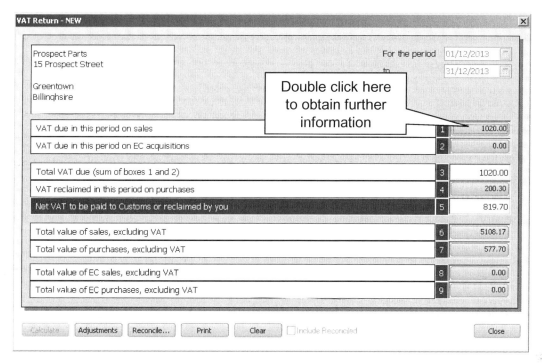

SAGE has now completed the VAT100 Form, as shown above. In order to check any of the entries, simply double-click on the figure and the breakdown of transactions that have been included in its calculation will be shown.

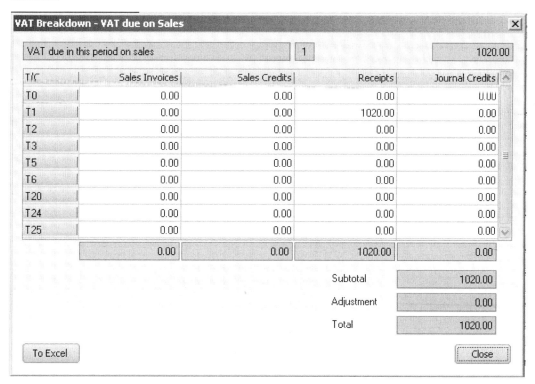

Here you can see the breakdown of figures used – each of these can be further investigated by double-clicking on the relevant cell.

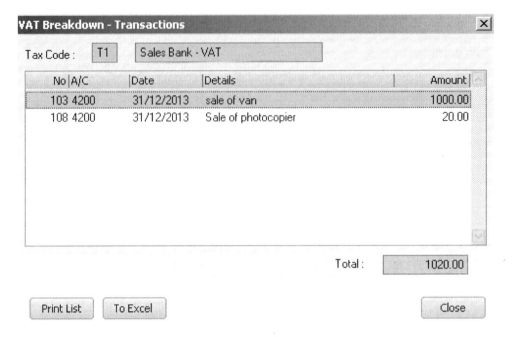

This shows the breakdown of the entries within the figure of £1020.00. You should now check the other entries against the manual check you did from the Audit Trail earlier. It is also useful to print a detailed report of all the items included in the VAT Return – this is done from the Print Button on VAT Return page. The detailed report should look like this (note this is only an extract).

Date: 28/01/2014   **Prospect Parts**   **Page:** 1
Time: 16:23:48   **VAT Report (Detailed)**

Date From: 01/10/2013   **Inc Current Reconciled:** No
Date To: 31/12/2013   **Inc Earlier Unreconciled:** No

Transactions Included In:
VAT Box 1   Receipts   Tax Code T1

No	Type	A/C	N/C	Ref	Date	Details	Amount	VR
103	BR	1200	4200		31/12/2013	sale of van	1,000.00	N
108	BR	1200	4200		31/12/2013	Sale of photocopier	20.00	N
						Total for Tax Code	1,020.00	
						Total for Vat Box 1	1,020.00	

Transactions Included In:
VAT Box 4   Payments   Tax Code T1

No	Type	A/C	N/C	Ref	Date	Details	Amount	VR
73	BP	1200	7550		31/12/2013	Tiny Telecom	12.62	N
98	BP	1200	0020	chq 027	31/12/2013	New machine	100.00	N
						Total for Tax Code	112.62	

Transactions Included In:
VAT Box 4   Journal Dbt   Tax Code T1

You can also print out a paper copy of the VAT return itself:

Date: 26/08/2014	**Prospect Parts**	Page: 1
Time: 11:43:59	**VAT Return**	

Date From: 01/12/2013		Inc Current	No
Date To: 31/12/2013		Inc Earlier	No

Transaction Number

Number of reconciled transactions included	0
Number of unreconciled transactions included (within date range)	7
Number of unreconciled transactions included (prior to date range)	0
Total number of transactions included	7

VAT due in this period on sales	1	1,020.00
VAT due in this period on EC acquisitions	2	0.00
Total VAT due (sum of boxes 1 and 2)	3	1,020.00
VAT reclaimed in this period on purchases	4	200.30
Net VAT to be paid to Customs or reclaimed by you	5	819.70
Total value of sales, excluding VAT	6	5,108.17
Total value of purchases, excluding VAT	7	577.70
Total value of EC sales, excluding VAT	8	0.00
Total value of EC purchases, excluding VAT	9	0.00

The VAT Return should then be reconciled (press the [Reconcile] button). Reconciling your transactions for VAT sets a flag against each transaction on the VAT Return. This flag indicates that the transaction has been included on a VAT Return, and so is excluded by default from subsequent VAT Returns.

In your audit trail the VAT column shows whether or not a transaction is reconciled. The letter R signifies that the transaction is reconciled; N signifies that the transaction is unreconciled; a hyphen or dash means that it is a non-VAT transaction, default tax code T9, or that its VAT code is one you have indicated is not to be included in calculating the VAT Return.

SAGE will also now give you the options shown below. This screen allows you to transfer the balances shown on N/C2200 Sales Tax Control and N/C2201 Purchase Tax Control to N/C2202 VAT liability.

You can then enter the payment made to HMRC which will be debited to N/C2202 VAT liability by SAGE to clear the VAT creditor for the quarter.

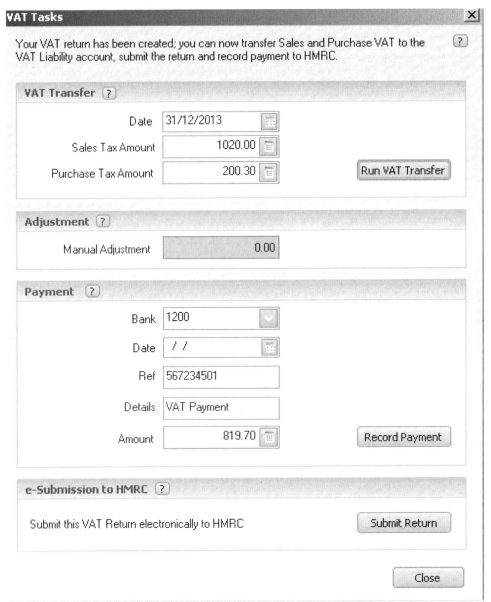

You have now completed your VAT reconciliation.

Final accounts for a sole trader

CONTENTS

1   Introduction
2   Suspense accounts and errors
3   Printing the Profit and Loss Account and the Balance Sheet
4   Year end procedures

1 Introduction

You have already printed out a number of trial balances for Prospect Parts The trial balance is one of the most useful reports that can be produced by a business, as it shows the current balances on each individual nominal account in the company's Chart of Accounts. The two columns of the trial balance (the *debit* column and the *credit* column) must always balance, and so the trial balance is a really useful and simple way of checking if there are any errors in the accounts.

2 Suspense accounts and errors

Where there is an error in the trial balance, SAGE will create an account called the *suspense account*. You can think of the suspense account as being like a cupboard under the stairs where things get put until you know what to do with them. Sage automatically creates a suspense account entry when it is unsure what to do with a particular transaction – for example, because of a coding error.

It is important that you regularly check the trial balance to ensure that there are no suspense account balances.

It is the bookkeeper's responsibility to clear out the suspense account so that errors or uncertainties are dealt with as quickly as possible. The usual way to clear out a suspense account in SAGE is by using a journal.

In the example shown below, it is apparent that there has been a mistake made in the data entry. SAGE has balanced the debits and credits by introducing a **SUSPENSE ACCOUNT** (Code 9998). On further inspection the bookkeeper has noticed that the figure for General Expenses (Code 8207) has been entered as £2855.64 instead of £1855.64. This must now be corrected.

There are a number of ways to make corrections in SAGE – one of the most common is via a **JOURNAL**. The journal can be found in **COMPANY** module. Here a correcting journal has been produced, crediting General Expenses (Code 8207) with £1000 and debiting Suspense Account (9998) with the same amount. Note that this journal is shown here for illustration purposes only and you should not enter this for the Prospect Parts case study in this study text.

 KAPLAN PUBLISHING

Example trial balance with suspense account

Date: 26/10/2011   **Wynn Bowlden Tennis Coach**   Page: 1
Time: 12:21:08   **Period Trial Balance**

To Period: Month 12, December 2011

N/C	Name	Debit	Credit
0030	Office Equipment	3,420.00	
0031	Office Equipment Depreciation		1,710.00
0050	Motor Vehicles	8,000.00	
0051	Motor Vehicles Depreciation		2,000.00
1001	Stock	2,865.90	
1100	Debtors Control Account	3,259.70	
1200	Bank Current Account	12,416.60	
1230	Petty Cash	100.00	
2100	Creditors Control Account		4,212.08
2202	VAT Liability		981.61
3000	Capital		3,500.00
3200	Profit and Loss Account		4,121.14
4000	Sales - Equipment		2,016.53
4001	Sales - Clothing and Footwear		2,195.46
4002	Sales - Individual Coaching		13,229.30
4003	Sales - Group Coaching		13,450.50
4004	Sales - Other		601.60
5000	Purchases - Equipment	1,015.20	
5001	Purchases - Clothing and Footwear	1,310.60	
5002	Purchases - Stationery	415.20	
5003	Purchases - Packaging	208.78	
5004	Purchases - Other Consumables	104.61	
7100	Rent	3,600.00	
7103	General Rates	350.00	
7304	Miscellaneous Motor Expenses	8,604.47	
7502	Telephone	491.52	
8207	General Expenses	2,855.64	
9998	Suspense Account		1,000.00
	Totals:	49,018.22	49,018.22

> Notice the suspense account indicating an error

Correcting Journal

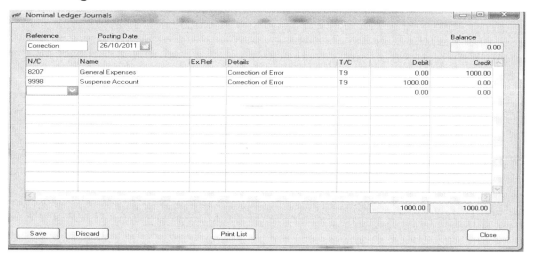

Amended trial balance

Date: 26/10/2011   **Wynn Bowlden Tennis Coach**   Page: 1
Time: 12:41:43   **Period Trial Balance**

To Period: Month 12, December 2011

N/C	Name	Debit	Credit
0030	Office Equipment	3,420.00	
0031	Office Equipment Depreciation		1,710.00
0050	Motor Vehicles	8,000.00	
0051	Motor Vehicles Depreciation		2,000.00
1001	Stock	2,865.90	
1100	Debtors Control Account	3,259.70	
1200	Bank Current Account	12,416.60	
1230	Petty Cash	100.00	
2100	Creditors Control Account		4,212.08
2202	VAT Liability		981.61
3000	Capital		3,500.00
3200	Profit and Loss Account		4,121.14
4000	Sales - Equipment		2,016.53
4001	Sales - Clothing and Footwear		2,195.46
4002	Sales - Individual Coaching		13,229.30
4003	Sales - Group Coaching		13,450.50
4004	Sales - Other		601.60
5000	Purchases - Equipment	1,015.20	
5001	Purchases - Clothing and Footwear	1,310.60	
5002	Purchases - Stationery	415.20	
5003	Purchases - Packaging	208.78	
5004	Purchases - Other Consumables	104.61	
7100	Rent	3,600.00	
7103	General Rates	350.00	
7304	Miscellaneous Motor Expenses	8,604.47	
7502	Telephone	491.52	
8207	General Expenses	1,855.64	
	Totals:	48,018.22	48,018.22

> The journal has corrected the error and there is no suspense account

Not all errors will be identified through the suspense account, however.

The following table shows which errors would not be identified in this way:

An **error of original entry**	Where both sides of a transaction include the wrong figure. For example, if a purchase invoice for £33 is entered as £35, this will result in an incorrect debit entry (to purchases), and an incorrect credit entry (to the relevant creditor account), both for £2 less. The total of both columns will be £2 less, and will thus balance – albeit incorrectly.

A **Transposition Error**	A particular type of error of original entry caused by putting two adjacent figures the wrong way round (e.g. 36 instead of 63). A top tip here is that any resulting difference will always be exactly divisible by 9.
An **error of omission**	Occurs when a transaction is completely omitted from the entries to the ledgers. As the entire transaction has been omitted, the trial balance would still balance.
An **error of reversal**	When entries are made for the correct amount, but with the debits and credits reversed. For example, if a cash purchase for £50 is debited to the Cash account, and credited to the Purchases account.
An **error of commission**	When entries are made for the correct amount, and the appropriate side (debit or credit), but one or more entries are made to the wrong account of the correct type – for example, the debit entry for the purchase of stamps being made against stationery costs instead of postage.
An **error of principle**	When the entries are made for the correct amount, and to the appropriate side (debit or credit), as with an error of commission, but the wrong **type** of account is used – a common example being to debit an *expense* account (e.g. purchases) with the costs of a purchase of an *asset* (e.g. machinery).
Compensating errors	These are multiple unrelated errors that would individually lead to an imbalance, but have the combined effect of cancelling each other out.

If you discover that your trial balance contains an unexpected error (or non-agreement) you should try to identify why this has happened. To do this you should:

- **Produce a Nominal Activity report** for the suspense account code (9998) – this will provide you with information about the balance on the suspense account.

- **Print an audit trail** of recent transactions – this will show you all your entries which you can then compare to the figures that should have been entered.

3 Printing the Profit and Loss Account and Balance Sheet

Once all of the transactions and any accounting adjustments for the year (e.g. depreciation, accruals and prepayments), you are ready to print off the Profit and Loss Account and the Balance Sheet to show the year end position of the business.

This is done from the Company – Financials module using the following icons:

Profit & Loss   Balance Sheet

Your reports should look like the ones shown below.

Date: 30/01/2014　　　　　　　**Prospect Parts**　　　　　　　**Page:** 1
Time: 13:58:28　　　　　　　　**Profit and Loss**

From:　　　Month 1, January 2013
To:　　　　Month 12, December 2013

Chart of Accounts:　　　　　Default Layout of Accounts

	Period		Year to Date	
Sales				
Product Sales	89,324.60		89,324.60	
Sales of Assets	(1,140.00)		(1,140.00)	
Other Sales	73.17		73.17	
		88,257.77		88,257.77
Purchases				
Purchases	57,082.46		57,082.46	
Stock	(490.00)		(490.00)	
		56,592.46		56,592.46
Direct Expenses				
		0.00		0.00
Gross Profit/(Loss):		31,665.31		31,665.31
Overheads				
Gross Wages	13,520.65		13,520.65	
Rent and Rates	2,095.62		2,095.62	
Motor Expenses	1,024.36		1,024.36	
Telephone and Computer charges	559.41		559.41	
Professional Fees	500.00		500.00	
Bank Charges and Interest	14.60		14.60	
Depreciation	4,655.00		4,655.00	
Bad Debts	476.55		476.55	
General Expenses	654.43		654.43	
		23,500.62		23,500.62
Net Profit/(Loss):		8,164.69		8,164.69

Date: 30/01/2014 Time: 13:59:47	**Prospect Parts** **Balance Sheet**		Page: 1	

From: Month 1, January 2013
To: Month 12, December 2013

Chart of Accounts: Default Layout of Accounts

	Period		Year to Date	
Fixed Assets				
Plant and Machinery	375.00		375.00	
Office Equipment	730.00		730.00	
Motor Vehicles	12,000.00		12,000.00	
		13,105.00		13,105.00
Current Assets				
Stock	1,390.00		1,390.00	
Debtors	1,547.04		1,547.04	
Deposits and Cash	300.00		300.00	
Bank Account	7,793.80		7,793.80	
		11,030.84		11,030.84
Current Liabilities				
Creditors : Short Term	4,208.12		4,208.12	
VAT Liability	1,767.20		1,767.20	
		5,975.32		5,975.32
Current Assets less Current Liabilities:		5,055.52		5,055.52
Total Assets less Current Liabilities:		18,160.52		18,160.52
Long Term Liabilities				
		0.00		0.00
Total Assets less Total Liabilities:		18,160.52		18,160.52
Capital & Reserves				
Capital	9,995.83		9,995.83	
P & L Account	8,164.69		8,164.69	
		18,160.52		18,160.52

4   Year end procedures

At the end of the financial year you need to transfer all of your balances from income and expenditure accounts to the profit and loss account, and then transfer the profit or loss for the year, as well as any capital introduced and drawings, to the capital account shown in the balance sheet. All income and expenditure account balances need to be zero for the start of the new financial year, whilst new opening balances need to be created in asset, liability and capital accounts to show the position at the start of the new financial year.

Before running the year end procedures in SAGE you should ensure you have taken two backup copies of your data, and printed all reports you require for the old financial year. You should then set your SAGE system date to the end of financial year date.

You will then need to select: Tools/Period End/Year end

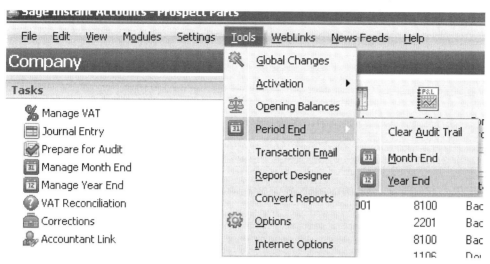

When you run the year end option, your software automatically resets to zero the balances of all your profit and loss nominal accounts for your new financial year.

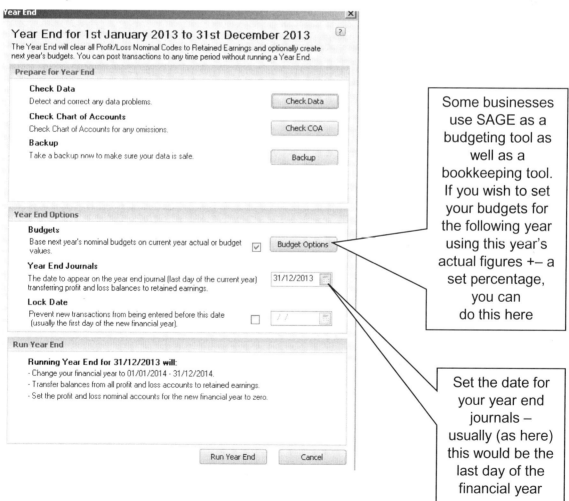

Some businesses use SAGE as a budgeting tool as well as a bookkeeping tool. If you wish to set your budgets for the following year using this year's actual figures +– a set percentage, you can do this here

Set the date for your year end journals – usually (as here) this would be the last day of the financial year

When SAGE has completed the year end procedure it will print out a report of all the journal entries it has made. You should file this carefully with all other supporting documentation for the year end.

The final adjustment to make now is to transfer both the drawings for the year ended 31st December 2013 shown in N/C3050 Drawings, and the profit or loss for the year shown in N/C3200 Profit and Loss Account, to the proprietor's capital account. Any capital introduced will also need to be transferred to the capital account – here there is none.

The totals for these two accounts should be taken from the opening trial balance at 1 January 2014, after carrying out the year end procedure above.

Date: 30/01/2014 **Prospect Parts** **Page:** 1
Time: 14:10:37

Period Trial Balance

To Period: Month 12, December 2014

N/C	Name	Debit	Credit
0020	Plant and Machinery	500.00	
0021	Plant/Machinery Depreciation		125.00
0030	Office Equipment	2,650.00	
0031	Office Equipment Depreciation		1,920.00
0050	Motor Vehicles	16,500.00	
0051	Motor Vehicles Depreciation		4,500.00
1001	Stock	1,390.00	
1100	Debtors Control Account	1,270.14	
1101	Accrued income	65.00	
1103	Prepayments	250.00	
1106	Provision for doubtful debts		38.10
1200	Bank Current Account	7,793.80	
1230	Petty Cash	300.00	
2100	Creditors Control Account		3,158.12
2109	Accruals		1,050.00
2202	VAT Liability		1,767.20
3000	Capital		15,715.83
3050	Drawings	5,720.00	
3200	Profit and Loss Account		8,164.69
	Totals:	36,438.94	36,438.94

The total drawings for the year, as well as any capital introduced, and the profit or loss for the year ended 31 December 2013 must now be transferred to the proprietor's capital account.

To transfer the balances for the year ended 31 December 2013 on N/C3050 Drawings and N/C3200 Profit and Loss Account, you will need to enter the following journal.

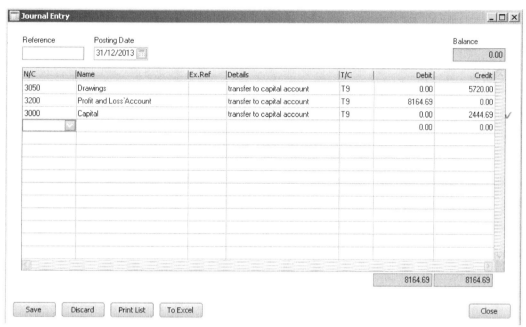

Note that the date of the journal should be 31st December 2013, as this is a transaction that occurs at the end of the year so that the opening capital account balance is correct at 1st January 2014. SAGE will generate the following warning message and you should choose "Yes".

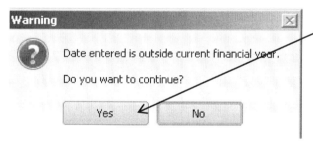

You should now print the trial balance at 1st January 2014 to show that the drawings, profit or loss for year (and any capital introduced where applicable) have been transferred to the proprietor's capital account.

Date: 30/01/2014   **Prospect Parts**   Page: 1
Time: 14:26:12   **Period Trial Balance**

To Period: Month 12, December 2014

N/C	Name	Debit	Credit
0020	Plant and Machinery	500.00	
0021	Plant/Machinery Depreciation		125.00
0030	Office Equipment	2,650.00	
0031	Office Equipment Depreciation		1,920.00
0050	Motor Vehicles	16,500.00	
0051	Motor Vehicles Depreciation		4,500.00
1001	Stock	1,390.00	
1100	Debtors Control Account	1,270.14	
1101	Accrued income	65.00	
1103	Prepayments	250.00	
1106	Provision for doubtful debts		38.10
1200	Bank Current Account	7,793.80	
1230	Petty Cash	300.00	
2100	Creditors Control Account		3,158.12
2109	Accruals		1,050.00
2202	VAT Liability		1,767.20
3000	Capital		18,160.52
	Totals:	30,718.94	30,718.94

The capital account balance of £18,160.52 is made up as follows:

N/C3000 Capital account (opening trial balance chapter 3)	15,715.83
N/C3050 Drawings (closing trial balance above)	(5,720.00)
N/C3200 Profit and loss account	8,164.69
N/C3000 capital account balance at 1st January 2014	18,160.52

Partnership accounts

CONTENTS

1 Introduction

A partnership exists where two or more people are carrying on a business with a view to make a profit.

Many of the accounting entries on SAGE for a partnership are the same as for a limited company.

The adjustments relating solely to partnership accounts are covered in this chapter.

The case study partnership used throughout this chapter is Tyrannosaurus Texts.

2 Background to the partnership

You are the bookkeeper for Tyrannosaurus Texts, a local bookshop. The owners of the business, Steph O'Saurus and Barry Onyx, have been trading as a partnership for 3 years. The year end, and today's date, is 31 December 2013.

The partnership details to enter on SAGE for Tyrannosaurus Texts are as follows:

Business Name:	Tyrannosaurus Texts
Business Address:	15 Rex Road Rex Town Ressex RE1 1TY
VAT Number:	234 5678 90
Financial Year:	1st January – 31st December

The opening trial balance for Tyrannosaurus Texts is given below:

Tyrannosaurus Texts

Opening Balances

	Nominal code	Debit	Credit
Freehold Property	0010	120000	
Furniture and Fittings	0040	8000	
Depreciation (Furniture/Fittings)	0041		3000
Stock (as at 1st January 2013)	1001	900	
Bank	1200	1500	
Petty Cash	1230	250	
Creditors Control Account	2100		2500
VAT Liability	2202		645
Steph O'Saurus Capital Account	3000		20000
Barry Onyx Capital Account	3001		15555
Steph O'Saurus Current Account	3060		2450
Barry Onyx Current Account	3061	2950	
Sales	4000		235500
Purchases	5000	105000	
Staff salaries	7003	32000	
Advertising	6201	4500	
General Rates	7103	3200	
Telephone	7550	650	
Sundry expenses	8250	700	
		279650	**279650**

Exercise

Enter the opening balance for each of the accounts.

Take care to enter each balance correctly and on the correct debit or credit side.

Note that the nominal codes above are appropriate for the standard partnership chart of accounts found in SAGEv19: if you are using the standard limited company chart of accounts, you will need to set up new nominal codes for the partners' current and capital accounts within the Capital and Reserves section.

Before you continue to enter transactions for Tyrannosaurus Texts, you should make sure that you have entered the opening trial balance correctly.

To do this, you will need to view the trial balance as at 31st December 2013 in the Company Financials screen and check all of the account balances are correct, and that no suspense account has been created by SAGE to balance the debits and credits you have entered.

If there are any errors in your trial balance at this stage, or if a suspense account has been created by SAGE as your debit and credit columns do not balance due to a mistake you have made, then you can correct these following the steps set out in chapter 2.

3 Adjustments and provisions

Many of the adjustments that need to be made in partnership accounts are the same as those that you have already learnt to make for limited company accounts in the earlier chapters.

These include:

- Clearing opening stock and entering closing stock
- Reversing opening accruals/prepayments and entering closing accruals/prepayments
- Providing for doubtful debts and writing off bad debts
- Accounting for fixed asset additions, disposals and depreciation

Exercise

Steph and Barry have valued the stock of Tyrannosaurus Texts at 31 December 2013 at a cost of £1,200.

Requirement:

Post the closing stock valuation on to SAGE.

Step One:

You will need to transfer the opening stock asset of £900 from the Balance Sheet Stock account N/C1001 to the opening stock account N/C5200 in the Profit and Loss Account.

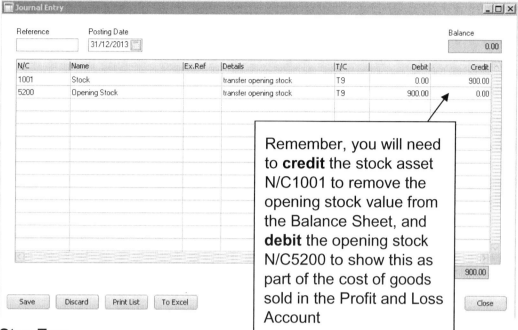

Remember, you will need to **credit** the stock asset N/C1001 to remove the opening stock value from the Balance Sheet, and **debit** the opening stock N/C5200 to show this as part of the cost of goods sold in the Profit and Loss Account

Step Two

You now need to record the value of the closing stock at the end of the year in both the Profit and Loss Account closing stock account N/C5201 and the Balance Sheet stock account N/C1001.

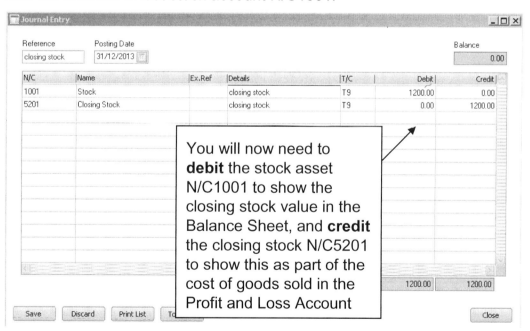

You will now need to **debit** the stock asset N/C1001 to show the closing stock value in the Balance Sheet, and **credit** the closing stock N/C5201 to show this as part of the cost of goods sold in the Profit and Loss Account

Once you have entered these journals, you should check the figures shown on the nominal ledger are all correct.

4 Profit-sharing arrangements in partnerships

The partnership agreement will set out how the profits of the business should be split between the partners. This could include:

- Salaries to be paid to partners

- Interest to be paid on capital account balances

- Interest to be charged on drawings

These are dealt with in turn below.

The balance of the profits, after adjusting for the above, will be split in accordance with the profit sharing ratio set out in the partnership agreement.

All of the above transactions will be treated as an appropriation of profits for the year and will be recorded in the partners' current accounts.

Before any of the above can be adjusted for, the Year End option must be run on SAGE.

This will generate the following year end report for the case study partnership:

Date: 07/02/2014						**Tyronnosaurus Texts**		**Page:** 1	
Time: 13:45:11						**Year End Report**			
No	**Item**	**Type**	**A/C**	**Date**	**Ref**	**Details**	**Net**	**Tax**	**Gross**
43	1	JD	4000	31/12/2013	Ledger	Ledger Year End	235,500.00	0.00	235,500.00
44	1	JC	5000	31/12/2013	Ledger	Ledger Year End	105,000.00	0.00	105,000.00
45	1	JC	5200	31/12/2013	Ledger	Ledger Year End	900.00	0.00	900.00
46	1	JD	5201	31/12/2013	Ledger	Ledger Year End	1,200.00	0.00	1,200.00
47	1	JC	6201	31/12/2013	Ledger	Ledger Year End	4,500.00	0.00	4,500.00
48	1	JC	7003	31/12/2013	Ledger	Ledger Year End	32,000.00	0.00	32,000.00
49	1	JC	7103	31/12/2013	Ledger	Ledger Year End	3,200.00	0.00	3,200.00
50	1	JC	7550	31/12/2013	Ledger	Ledger Year End	650.00	0.00	650.00
51	1	JC	8250	31/12/2013	Ledger	Ledger Year End	700.00	0.00	700.00
52	1	JC	3200	31/12/2013	Ledger	Ledger Year End	89,750.00	0.00	89,750.00

Note that there is a total profit for the year of £89,750. We will split this between the two partners in the following sections.

5 Interest on capital and drawings

Interest on Capital

When a partnership is entered into, the partners will need to make an agreement as to how much capital each will introduce into the business. This could be in the form of cash or assets introduced, and will be shown in the relevant partner's capital account.

Looking at the opening trial balance for Tyrannosaurus Texts, you can see that Steph has a capital account with a credit balance of £20,000 and Barry has one with a credit balance of £15,555.

It is common for notional interest to be paid on this capital introduced in order to compensate those partners who contribute a larger share of the capital to the partnership. The rate of interest to be paid on the capital accounts will be set out in the partnership agreement.

Any interest paid on capital account balances will be deducted **(debited)** from retained profits in N/C3200 and **credited** to the appropriate partner's current account (as income for the partner).

Exercise

The partnership agreement of Tyrannosaurus Texts states that interest should be paid on capital at a rate of 7% p.a.

Requirement:

Enter the interest on capital on SAGE.

interest on capital

Steph 1400

Barry 1089

Solution

Interest should be paid as follows:

Steph: £20,000 × 7% = £1,400

Barry: £15,555 × 7% = £1,089

This will be **debited** to N/C3200 Profit and Loss Account to reduce the retained profits of the partnership, and **credited** to N/C3060 and N/C3061 to increase the partners' current accounts.

You will need to post the journal shown below on SAGE:

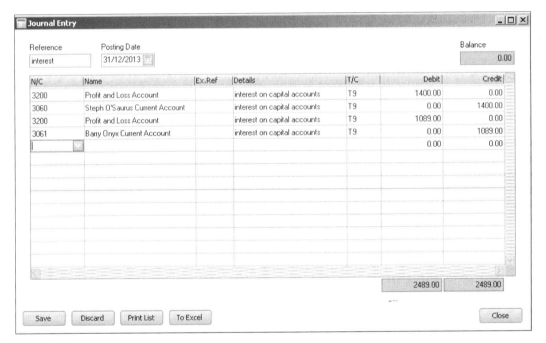

Note that when you post this journal, and the ones below, you will see the following message:

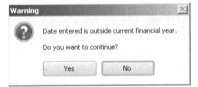

This message appears because you have already run the year end and are posting a journal dated 31 December 2013. You should click on "Yes" to continue posting the transaction.

Interest on Drawings

There is sometimes a provision in the partnership agreement for notional interest to be charged on drawings made by each partner: this is so that those partners who draw more money early in the financial year suffer a financial cost for doing so.

This is dealt with in a similar way to interest on capital accounts:

The interest charged on drawings will be **debited** to the partners' current accounts (as a cost to the partner), and **credited** to N/C3200 Profit and Loss Account.

Exercise

The partnership agreement of Tyrannosaurus Texts states that interest should be paid on drawings at a rate of 8% p.a.

Drawings for the year to 31 December 2013 (included within the current account balances shown on the opening trial balance) are:

Steph	1 June 2012	£10,000
Barry	1 September 2012	£8,000

Requirement

Enter the notional interest charge on drawings on SAGE.

467
213

Solution

Interest should be charged as follows:

Steph: £10,000 × 8% × 7/12 = £467

Barry: £8,000 × 8% = 4/12 = £213

This will be **debited** to N/C3060 and N/C3061 to reduce the partners' current account balances and **credited** to N/C3200 Profit and Loss Account to increase the retained profits of the partnership.

You will need to post the journal shown below on SAGE:

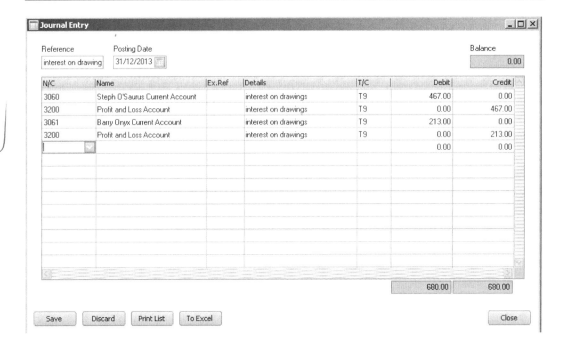

6 Partners' salaries

Where partners receive a fixed salary as part of the partnership agreement, you will need to remember that this should also be treated as an appropriation of profit: this is in contrast to an employee salary which is treated as an expense in the Profit and Loss Account.

The salary will be **debited** to N/C3200 to reduce the retained profits for the year, and is then credited to the partner's current account, as this is money owed to the partner by the partnership.

When the partner withdraws the salary, this is then treated as normal cash drawings.

Exercise

The partnership agreement of Tyrannosaurus Texts states that Steph is entitled to a salary of £5,000 per annum. Steph draws this salary on 1 February 2014.

Requirement

Enter the salary on SAGE.

Solution

The salary of £5,000 will be debited to N/C 3200 to reduce the retained profits of the partnership, and credited to N/C3060 to increase Steph's current account balance.

The salary has not been paid as at 31 December 2013, so you do not need to make any further entries on SAGE for the bank payment.

You will need to post the journal shown below on SAGE.

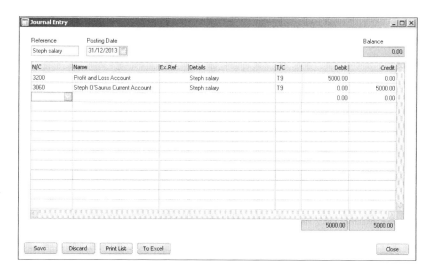

7 Allocating net profit and profit-sharing ratios

Any remaining profit for the year is shared between the partners according to the terms set out in the partnership agreement.

The remaining profit for the year can be seen by examining N/C3200. Looking at the trial balance for Tyrannosaurus Texts, N/C3200 shows a balance of £82,941 CR.

This is made up as shown in the profit appropriation account shown below:

Profit appropriation account

Profit for the year per the year-end report	89,750
Interest paid to Steph	(1,400)
Interest paid to Barry	(1,089)
Interest charged on drawings: Steph	467
Interest charged on drawings: Barry	213
Steph's salary	(5,000)
Remaining profit for the year	82,941

Exercise

The partnership agreement of Tyrannosaurus Texts states that the balance of profit or loss for the year is to be divided between Steph and Barry in the ratio 3:2.

Requirement

Allocate the remaining profit for the year between the two partners on SAGE.

Solution

Steph is entitled to 3/5 × £82,941 = £49,765

Barry is entitled to 2/5 × £82,941 = £33,176

The profit share for each partner will be **debited** to N/C3200 and **credited** to that partner's current account.

You will now need to enter the journal shown below on SAGE.

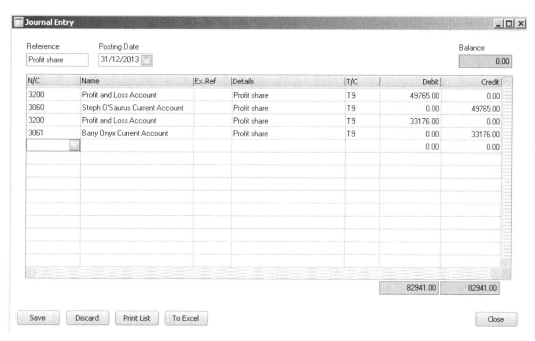

To check that you have correctly allocated the profit for the year you should choose to view the breakdown of Capital and Reserves shown on the Balance Sheet on SAGE, and compare this with the extract shown below.

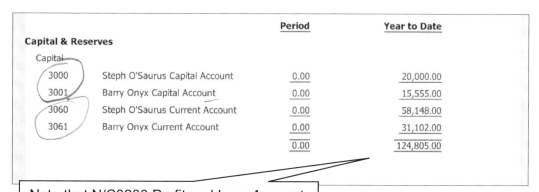

Note that N/C3200 Profit and Loss Account does not appear as part of Capital and Reserves, as you have successfully allocated the profit for the year between the two partners

8 Extracting the Balance Sheet

You should now print out a copy of the Balance Sheet to show the opening balances at 1st January 2014. This can be done from the Company Financials screen.

Your report should look like the one shown below:

Date: 07/02/2014	**Tyronnosaurus Texts**		**Page:** 1
Time: 13:57:44	**Balance Sheet**		

From: Month 1, January 2014
To: Month 12, December 2014

Chart of Accounts: Default Layout of Accounts

	Period		Year to Date	
Fixed Assets				
Property	0.00		120,000.00	
Furniture and Fixtures	0.00		5,000.00	
		0.00		125,000.00
Current Assets				
Stock	0.00		1,200.00	
Deposits and Cash	0.00		250.00	
Bank Account	0.00		1,500.00	
		0.00		2,950.00
Current Liabilities				
Creditors : Short Term	0.00		2,500.00	
VAT Liability	0.00		645.00	
		0.00		3,145.00
Current Assets less Current Liabilities:		0.00		(195.00)
Total Assets less Current Liabilities:		0.00		124,805.00
Long Term Liabilities				
		0.00		0.00
Total Assets less Total Liabilities:		0.00		124,805.00
Capital & Reserves				
Capital	0.00		124,805.00	
P & L Account	0.00		0.00	
		0.00		124,805.00

9   Revaluations of tangible fixed assets

Where a tangible fixed asset is revalued by a partnership, the following steps should be followed:

Step one: Enter the revaluation in the revaluation reserve

Step two: Transfer the balance on the revaluation reserve to the partners' capital accounts in accordance with the profit-sharing ratio.

0010 Dt 50.

Example

On 1st January 2014, Steph and Barry decide to revalue the freehold property to its current market value of £150,000.

To enter the revaluation, the following journal would be entered on SAGE:

DR N/C0010 Freehold Property   £30,000

CR N/C   Revaluation reserve £30,000

The balance on the revaluation reserve would then be split in accordance with the profit-sharing ratio set out in the partnership agreement of Tyrannosaurus Texts. This states that profits should be shared between Steph and Barry in the ratio 3:2.

Therefore the portion of the revaluation to credit to Steph's capital account would be £18,000, and Barry would be credited with £12,000.

This would be entered on SAGE as follows:

DR N/C3101 Revaluation reserve   £30,000

CR N/C3000 Steph capital account   £18,000 ✓

CR N/C3001 Barry capital account   £12,000 ✓

Not for profit organisations

CONTENTS

1 Introduction

Not for profit organisations are organisations which do not distribute their excess profits to members but instead use them to further the activities of the organisation.

Common examples include charities, clubs and societies.

Transactions for Not for Profit Organisations are usually entered on SAGE on a cash receipts basis, and then adjustments are made at the end of the financial period for accruals, prepayments and depreciation.

At the end of the financial period, an Income and Expenditure Account and a Balance Sheet are prepared for presentation to the members.

The Income and Expenditure Account will show receipts and payments for the year, adjusted for any accruals.

The Balance Sheet will show the Accumulated Fund at the year end. This represents the members' interest in the club or society and is equivalent to Assets less Liabilities.

> **Assets less Liabilities = Accumulated Fund**

2 Background to the organisation

You are the book-keeper for Goldhill Community Golf Club and are preparing the accounts for the year ended 31 March 2013. The club provides golf lessons and social facilities for the local community and is a not-for-profit organisation. Goldhill Community Golf Club is funded partly through membership subscriptions, and partly by social events and donations.

The club is not registered for VAT.

The opening Trial Balance for Goldhill Community Golf Club is given below. The default chart of accounts for not for profit organisations in SAGEv19 has been used.

Goldhill Community Golf Club

Opening Balances

	Nominal code	Debit	Credit
Golf Club Premises	0010	80000	
Golf Club Premises Depreciation	0011		8000
Furniture and Fittings	0040	4000	
Depreciation (Furniture/Fittings)	0041		1200
Bank	1200	750	
Petty Cash	1230	50	
Accumulated Fund	3200		38250
Income: Bar Sales	4400		17000
Income: Raffle	4500		1550
Income: Sponsorship	4800		2450
Income: Members' Subscriptions	4900		55000
Purchases: Bar	5001	14500	
Purchases: Sundry	5002	3850	
Advertising	6101	1200	
General Rates	7003	1700	
Telephone	7350	250	
Insurance	7604	800	
Sundry expenses	7606	300	
Staff salaries	7803	16050	
		123450	**123450**

Note that for not-for-profit organisations, the Accumulated Fund represents the members' interests in the club or society

Enter the opening balance for each of the accounts.

Take care to enter each balance correctly and on the correct debit or credit side.

Before you continue to enter transactions for Goldhill Community Golf Club, you should make sure that you have entered the opening trial balance correctly.

Date:	08/07/2013	**Goldhill Community Golf Club**		Page: 1
Time:	17:34:19	**Period Trial Balance**		

To Period: Month 12, March 2013

N/C	Name	Debit	Credit
0010	Golf Club Premises	80,000.00	
0011	Golf Club Premises Depreciation		8,000.00
0040	Furniture and Fixtures	4,000.00	
0041	Furniture/Fixture Depreciation		1,200.00
1200	Bank Current Account	750.00	
1230	Petty Cash	50.00	
3200	Accumulated Fund		38,250.00
4400	Bar Sales		17,000.00
4500	Raffle		1,550.00
4800	Sponsorship		2,450.00
4900	Members' Subscriptions		55,000.00
5001	Purchases - Bar	14,500.00	
5002	Purchases- Sundry	3,850.00	
6101	Advertising	1,200.00	
7003	General Rates	1,700.00	
7350	Telephone	250.00	
7604	Insurance	800.00	
7606	Sundry Expenses	300.00	
7803	Staff Salaries	16,050.00	
	Totals:	123,450.00	123,450.00

If there are any errors in your trial balance at this stage, or if a suspense account has been created by SAGE as your debit and credit columns do not balance due to a mistake you have made, then you can correct these using a journal entry.

3 Adjustments and provisions

Many of the adjustments that need to be made for not-for-profit organisations are the same as those that you have already learnt to make for sole trader accounts in the earlier chapters.

These include:

- Clearing opening stock and entering closing stock
- Reversing opening accruals/prepayments and entering closing accruals/prepayments (covered in detail in the next section)
- Providing for doubtful debts and writing off bad debts
- Accounting for fixed asset additions, disposals and depreciation.

Exercise

Goldhill Community Golf Club depreciates its tangible fixed assets on the following bases:

Golf Club Premises – 5% per annum on a straight line basis.

Furniture and Fixtures – 25% per annum on a reducing balance basis.

Requirement

Calculate the depreciation charge for each class of fixed assets for the year and enter this on SAGE.

Step one: Using the balances shown on the nominal ledger, calculate the depreciation charge for each class of asset.

Golf Club Premises: N/C0010 Golf Club Premises shows a total cost of £80,000.

The depreciation charge for the year for the Golf Club Premises will be £80,000 × 5% = £4,000.

Furniture and Fixtures: N/C0040 Furniture and Fixtures shows a total cost of £4,000, and N/C0041 Furniture and Fixtures Depreciation shows a total accumulated depreciation of £1,200, giving a net book value of £2,800.

The depreciation charge for the year for furniture and fixtures will be 25% × £2,800 = £700.

We will **debit** the relevant depreciation expense accounts N/C8000 – N/C8004 with the depreciation charge for the year. This will be shown as the total depreciation expense in the Profit and Loss Account for the year.

We will **credit** the relevant accumulated depreciation accounts N/C0011 and N/C0041, with the depreciation charge for the year. These are Balance Sheet accounts and so show the cumulative depreciation charged to date for each class of assets. These accumulated depreciation accounts will reduce the cost of the fixed assets shown in the Balance Sheet.

The journal to enter the depreciation charge on SAGE is shown below:

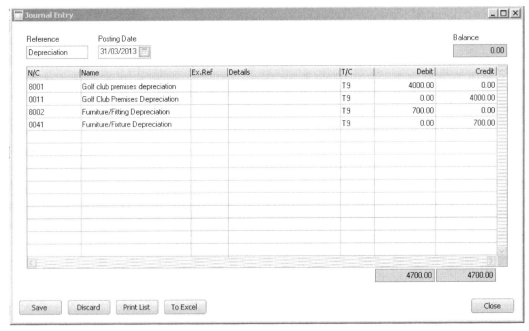

4 Donations and subscriptions

With not-for-profit organisations, subscriptions and donations are entered on SAGE when they are received. It is often the case that, at the end of the year, members' subscriptions have been paid in advance or arrears. You will need to adjust for these on SAGE in the same way as for accruals and prepayments for a sole trader.

Subscriptions received **in advance** of the accounting period to which they relate will have been entered on SAGE and so the Income and Expenditure Account will show income that relates to a future accounting period.

In order to adjust for subscriptions received in advance on SAGE, you will need to input a journal which decreases the relevant income account in the Income and Expenditure Account, and shows a current liability for subscriptions in advance in the Balance Sheet.

Subscriptions received **in arrears** after the accounting period to which they relate will not have been entered on SAGE and so will not be included as income in the Income and Expenditure Account.

In order to adjust for subscriptions received in arrears on SAGE, you will need to post a journal which increases the relevant income account in the Income and Expenditure Account, and shows a current asset for subscriptions in arrears in the Balance Sheet.

CASE STUDY

The membership fee of the Golf Club is £110 per year, and memberships run from 1 April one year to 31 March the next year.

At 31 March 2013, 6 members had not paid their subscription for the year ended 31 March 2013. 3 members had already paid their subscription for the year ended 31 March 2014.

Requirement

Adjust for the subscriptions paid in advance and in arrears at 31 March 2013.

arrears - 6 × 110 = 660
in advance - 3 × 110 = 330

Solution

Subscriptions paid in arrears: 6 members had not paid their subscriptions at 31 March 2013. This is a total of 6 × £110 = £660 paid in arrears.

To adjust for this on SAGE, we will need to debit N/C1102 Subs in arrears to show the money owed to the club as part of current assets in the Balance Sheet, and also credit N/C4900 Members' Subscriptions to show the income which has not been entered in the Income and Expenditure Account.

Subscriptions paid in advance: 3 members had paid their subscriptions for the following year at 31 March 2013. This is a total of 3 × £110 = £330 paid in advance.

To adjust for this on SAGE, we will need to debit N/C4900 Members' Subscriptions to remove the income which has been entered in the Income and Expenditure Account, and also credit N/C2101 Subscriptions in advance to show the money received in advance as part of current liabilities in the Balance Sheet.

Note that you will need to rename these nominal accounts in the default chart of accounts.

Check your journal against the ones shown below:

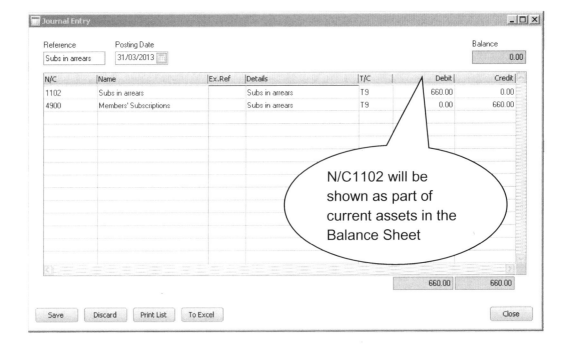

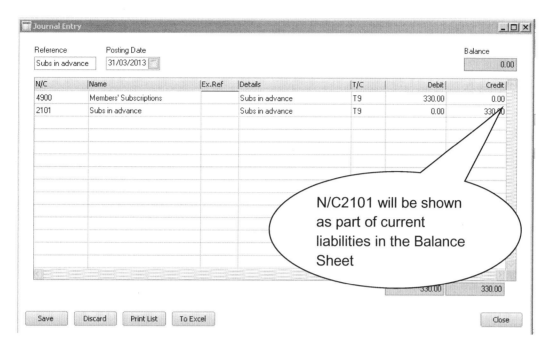

After posting these journals, your trial balance should look like this:

Date: 08/07/2013   **Goldhill Community Golf Club**   Page: 1
Time: 20:57:17   **Period Trial Balance**

To Period: Month 12, March 2013

N/C	Name	Debit	Credit
0010	Golf Club Premises	80,000.00	
0011	Golf Club Premises Depreciation		12,000.00
0040	Furniture and Fixtures	4,000.00	
0041	Furniture/Fixture Depreciation		1,900.00
1102	Subs in arrears	660.00	
1200	Bank Current Account	750.00	
1230	Petty Cash	50.00	
2101	Subs in advance		330.00
3200	Accumulated Fund		38,250.00
4400	Bar Sales		17,000.00
4500	Raffle		1,550.00
4800	Sponsorship		2,450.00
4900	Members' Subscriptions		55,330.00
5001	Purchases - Bar	14,500.00	
5002	Purchases- Sundry	3,850.00	
6101	Advertising	1,200.00	
7003	General Rates	1,700.00	
7350	Telephone	250.00	
7604	Insurance	800.00	
7606	Sundry Expenses	300.00	
7803	Staff Salaries	16,050.00	
8001	Golf club premises depreciation	4,000.00	
8002	Furniture/Fitting Depreciation	700.00	
	Totals:	128,810.00	128,810.00

5 Extracting the Income and Expenditure Report and the Balance Sheet

You should now print out a copy of the Income and Expenditure Report and the Balance Sheet showing all of the adjustments you have put through. This can be done from the Company Financials screen. Note that you will need to rename headings within the default chart of accounts on SAGE as appropriate. Your reports should look like this:

Date: 08/07/2013	**Goldhill Community Golf Club**		**Page:** 1	
Time: 21:08:54	**Balance Sheet**			
From: Month 1, April 2012				
To: Month 12, March 2013				
Chart of Accounts:	Default Layout of Accounts			
	Period		**Year to Date**	
Fixed Assets				
Property	68,000.00		68,000.00	
Furniture and Fixtures	2,100.00		2,100.00	
		70,100.00		70,100.00
Current Assets				
Debtors	660.00		660.00	
Deposits and Cash	50.00		50.00	
Bank Account	750.00		750.00	
		1,460.00		1,460.00
Current Liabilities				
Creditors : Short Term	330.00		330.00	
		330.00		330.00
Current Assets less Current Liabilities:		1,130.00		1,130.00
Total Assets less Current Liabilities:		71,230.00		71,230.00
Long Term Liabilities				
		0.00		0.00
Total Assets less Total Liabilities:		71,230.00		71,230.00
Capital & Reserves				
Accumulated Fund	38,250.00		38,250.00	
P & L Account	32,980.00		32,980.00	
		71,230.00		71,230.00

Date: 08/07/2013	**Goldhill Community Golf Club**	Page: 1
Time: 21:14:57	**Profit and Loss**	

From: Month 1, April 2012
To: Month 12, March 2013

Chart of Accounts: Default Layout of Accounts

	Period		Year to Date	
Sales				
Bar Sales	17,000.00		17,000.00	
Raffle	1,550.00		1,550.00	
Sponsorship	2,450.00		2,450.00	
Members' subscriptions	55,330.00		55,330.00	
		76,330.00		76,330.00
Purchases				
Purchases	18,350.00		18,350.00	
		18,350.00		18,350.00
Direct Expenses				
Advertising	1,200.00		1,200.00	
		1,200.00		1,200.00
Gross Profit/(Loss):		56,780.00		56,780.00
Overheads				
Rent and Rates	1,700.00		1,700.00	
Telephone and Computer charges	250.00		250.00	
General Expenses	1,100.00		1,100.00	
Gross Wages	16,050.00		16,050.00	
Depreciation	4,700.00		4,700.00	
		23,800.00		23,800.00
Net Profit/(Loss):		32,980.00		32,980.00

In your ICB exam, you should make every effort to use appropriate headings and nominal account codes when preparing accounts for a not for profit organisation. However, you will not be penalised if your software package does not completely facilitate this: the ICB do ask that you write a note on your initial Balance Sheet indicating the software you have used so this can be taken into account when marking your assessment.

6   Year-end procedures

At the end of the financial year you need to transfer all of your balances from income and expenditure accounts to the profit and loss account: this will give you the excess of income over expenditure (or excess of expenditure over income) for the year which will be transferred to the accumulated fund account shown in the balance sheet.

All income and expenditure account balances need to be zero for the start of the new financial year, whilst new opening balances need to be created in asset, liability and capital accounts to show the position at the start of the new financial year.

Before running the year end procedures in SAGE you should ensure you have taken two backup copies of your data, and printed all reports you require for the old financial year. You should then set your SAGE system date to the end of financial year date.

You will then need to select: Tools/Period End/Year end and run the year end procedure as set out in chapter 11.

Practice assessment

CONTENTS

1 Practice assessment

The scenario

You are the book-keeper for Hair Care Supplies, a partnership which supplies shampoo and other hair care products to salons: you are preparing the accounts for the year ended 31 March 2013. Today's date is 31 March 2013.

Keith Thompson, Annabel Harrison and Harley Clifford are the three founding partners.

The partnership is registered for VAT.

Partnership Agreement

Since the formation of the partnership, profits have been shared using the ratio of 2:2:1, with Harley receiving 20% of the profits. You should assume that all profits are earned evenly throughout the year.

Annabel will be paid a salary of £4,000 p.a. from 1 November 2012 onwards.

Fixed Assets

2 computers were scrapped in the year for nil proceeds. These are shown in the accounts at a cost of £500 each, and with £300 accumulated depreciation each.

Depreciation

The partnership's depreciation policy is as follows:

Motor Vehicles – 25% per annum on a reducing balance basis

Computer Equipment – 30% per annum on a reducing balance basis

Fixtures and Fittings – 20 % per annum on a straight line basis

A full year's depreciation is charged in the year of acquisition, and none in the year of disposal.

Initial Trial Balance as at 31 March 2013

The initial trial balance for Hair Care Supplies is given below:

	Debit	Credit
Computer Equipment	4000	
Computer Equipment Depreciation		2500
Furniture and Fittings	4175	
Depreciation (Furniture/Fittings)		1075
Motor Vehicles	30500	
Motor Vehicles Depreciation		2500
Stock	34050	
Debtors control account	12500	
Prepayments (rent)	200	
Provision for doubtful debts		475
Bank	1350	
Creditors control account		6575
Accruals (advertising)		350
VAT liability		2500
Keith Thompson Capital Account		10000
Annabel Harrison Capital Account		10000
Harley Clifford Capital Account		5000
Keith Thompson Current Account	1250	
Annabel Harrison Current Account		3050
Harley Clifford Current Account		2500
Sales		220000
Purchases	150000	
Advertising	1400	
Staff salaries	22000	
Rent	1300	
Rates	600	
Electricity	450	
Telephone	650	
Motor expenses	1300	
Insurance	200	
Sundry expenses	250	
Repairs	350	
	266525	**266525**

Adjustments

Rent is paid in advance. £400 in respect of rent for the 4 months ending 30 June 2013 was paid on 1 March 2013.

An accrual of £300 is needed for advertising expenses.

Closing stock has been valued at £12,000.

The provision for doubtful debts should be 1% of the total trade debtors balances.

Section One (70 marks)

Task 1

Post the initial trial balance on to SAGE, creating new nominal codes where applicable.

Print the following reports and label them with the task number:

- Initial Trial Balance
- Initial Balance Sheet
- Initial Profit and Loss Account

(10 marks)

Task 2

Adjustments:

(1) Post the necessary journals for the rent prepayment

(5 marks)

(2) Post the necessary journals for the advertising accrual

(5 marks)

(3) Post the required transactions for the change in the provision for doubtful debts

(5 marks)

(4) Enter the journal necessary to deal with the computers scrapped in the year

(5 marks)

(5) Calculate and post the depreciation charge for the year

(5 marks)

(6) Post the closing stock valuation

(5 marks)

(7) Print the following reports:

- Draft Trial Balance

- Draft Balance Sheet

- Draft Profit and Loss Account

(10 marks)

Task 3

Process the year-end and make the necessary adjustments to share the profit in accordance with the Partnership Agreement.

(10 marks)

Task 4

Print the following reports:

- An Opening Balance Sheet as at 1 April 2013

- An Opening Trial Balance as at 1 April 2013

(10 marks)

2 Practice assessment answers

Section One

Task 1

Your initial Trial Balance, Balance Sheet and Profit and Loss Account should agree to the ones below:

Date: 09/07/2013
Time: 11:34:52

Hair Care Supplies Ltd
Period Trial Balance

Page: 1

To Period: Month 12, March 2013

N/C	Name	Debit	Credit
0030	Computer Equipment	4,000.00	
0031	Computer Equipment Depreciation		2,500.00
0040	Furniture and Fixtures	4,175.00	
0041	Furniture/Fixture Depreciation		1,075.00
0050	Motor Vehicles	30,500.00	
0051	Motor Vehicles Depreciation		2,500.00
1001	Stock	34,050.00	
1100	Debtors Control Account	12,500.00	
1103	Prepayments	200.00	
1106	Provision for doubtful debts		475.00
1200	Bank Current Account	1,350.00	
2100	Creditors Control Account		6,575.00
2109	Accruals		350.00
2202	VAT Liability		2,500.00
3000	Keith Thompson Capital Account		10,000.00
3001	Annabel Harrison Capital Account		10,000.00
3002	Harley Clifford Capital Account		5,000.00
3060	Keith Thompson Current Account	1,250.00	
3061	Annabel Harrison Current Account		3,050.00
3062	Harley Clifford Capital Account		2,500.00
4000	Sales		220,000.00
5000	Purchases	150,000.00	
6201	Advertising	1,400.00	
7003	Staff Salaries	22,000.00	
7100	Rent	1,300.00	
7103	General Rates	600.00	
7200	Electricity	450.00	
7304	Miscellaneous Motor Expenses	1,300.00	
7550	Telephone and Fax	650.00	
7800	Repairs and Renewals	350.00	
8204	Insurance	200.00	
8250	Sundry Expenses	250.00	
	Totals:	266,525.00	266,525.00

Date: 09/07/2013
Time: 11:37:58

Hair Care Supplies Ltd
Balance Sheet

Page: 1

From: Month 1, April 2012
To: Month 12, March 2013

Chart of Accounts: Default Layout of Accounts

	Period		Year to Date	
Fixed Assets				
Office Equipment	1,500.00		1,500.00	
Furniture and Fixtures	3,100.00		3,100.00	
Motor Vehicles	28,000.00		28,000.00	
		32,600.00		32,600.00
Current Assets				
Stock	34,050.00		34,050.00	
Debtors	12,225.00		12,225.00	
Bank Account	1,350.00		1,350.00	
		47,625.00		47,625.00
Current Liabilities				
Creditors : Short Term	6,925.00		6,925.00	
VAT Liability	2,500.00		2,500.00	
		9,425.00		9,425.00
Current Assets less Current Liabilities:		38,200.00		38,200.00
Total Assets less Current Liabilities:		70,800.00		70,800.00
Long Term Liabilities				
		0.00		0.00
Total Assets less Total Liabilities:		70,800.00		70,800.00
Capital & Reserves				
Capital	29,300.00		29,300.00	
P & L Account	41,500.00		41,500.00	
		70,800.00		70,800.00

Date: 09/07/2013
Time: 11:39:27

Hair Care Supplies Ltd
Profit and Loss

Page: 1

From: Month 1, April 2012
To: Month 12, March 2013

Chart of Accounts: Default Layout of Accounts

	Period		Year to Date	
Sales				
Product Sales	220,000.00		220,000.00	
		220,000.00		220,000.00
Purchases				
Purchases	150,000.00		150,000.00	
		150,000.00		150,000.00
Direct Expenses				
Sales Promotion	1,400.00		1,400.00	
		1,400.00		1,400.00
Gross Profit/(Loss):		68,600.00		68,600.00
Overheads				
Gross Wages	22,000.00		22,000.00	
Rent and Rates	1,900.00		1,900.00	
Heat, Light and Power	450.00		450.00	
Motor Expenses	1,300.00		1,300.00	
Telephone and Computer charges	650.00		650.00	
Maintenance	350.00		350.00	
General Expenses	450.00		450.00	
		27,100.00		27,100.00
Net Profit/(Loss):		41,500.00		41,500.00

Task 2

(1) Before entering the closing rent prepayment, you will need to reverse the opening rent prepayment shown in the initial trial balance.

Rent of £400 has been paid on 1 March 2013 for the 4 months ending 30 June 2013. Therefore, the closing rent prepayment will be: £400 × 3/4 = £300.

The journals to adjust the rent prepayment are:

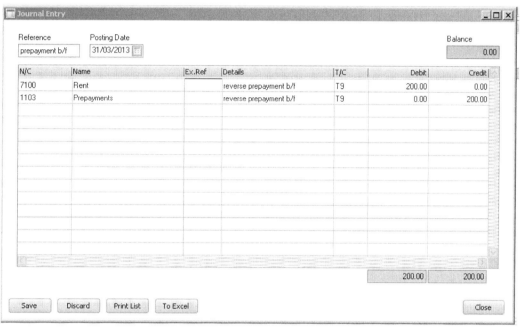

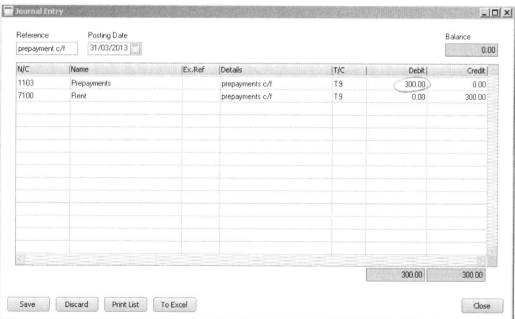

(2) Before entering the closing advertising accrual, you will need to reverse the opening advertising accrual shown in the initial trial balance.

You can then enter the closing accrual of £300, given to you in the question.

The journals to adjust the advertising accrual are:

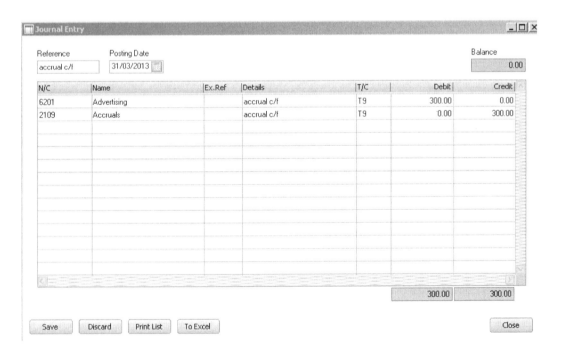

(3) The provision for doubtful debts at 31 March 2013 should be 1% of the total trade debtors balances, i.e. 1% × £12,500 = £1,250. The initial Trial Balance shows a provision for doubtful debts of £475: you will need to enter a journal to increase this provision by £775 at the year end.

The journal to increase the bad debt provision is shown below:

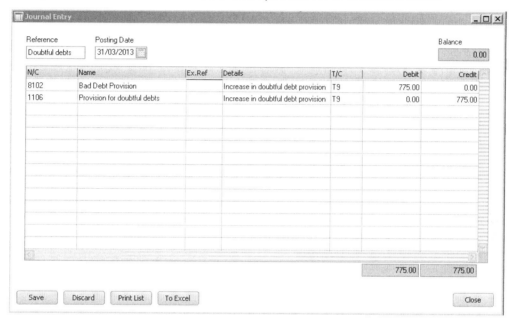

(4) The cost and the accumulated depreciation in respect of the computers scrapped in the year will need to be transferred to the disposals account in the Profit and Loss Account, as per the journal below:

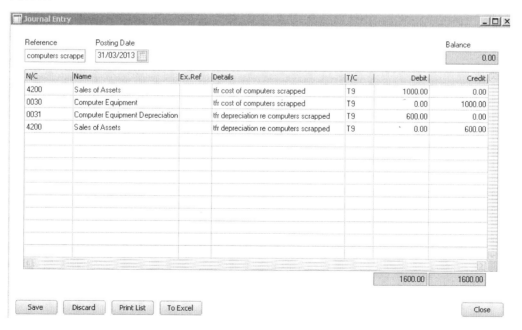

(5) The depreciation charge for the year will be as follows:

Motor Vehicles: £30,500 – £2,500 = £28,000 × 25% = £7,000

Computer Equipment: £3,000 – £1,900 = £1,100 × 30% = £330

Fixtures and Fittings: £4,175 × 20% = £835

The journal to enter the depreciation charge is shown below. Note that the entries to N/C8000 have been shown as one total figure. These could also be shown as individual entries to N/C8000.

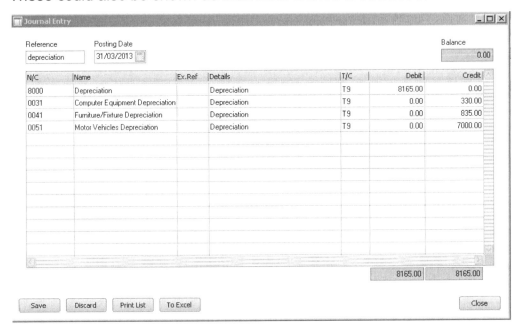

(6)   Before entering the closing stock figure, you will need to transfer the opening stock figure from the Balance Sheet stock account to the Profit and Loss opening stock account, using the following journal:

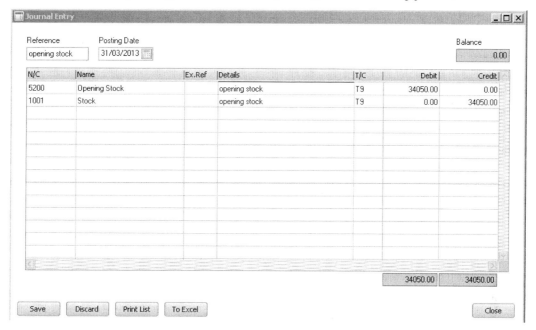

You can then enter the closing stock figure, as shown below:

(7) Your draft Trial Balance, Balance Sheet and Profit and Loss Account should agree to the ones shown below:

Date: 09/07/2013	**Hair Care Supplies Ltd**		**Page:** 1
Time: 12:44:06	**Period Trial Balance**		

To Period: Month 12, March 2013

N/C	Name	Debit	Credit
0030	Computer Equipment	3,000.00	
0031	Computer Equipment Depreciation		2,230.00
0040	Furniture and Fixtures	4,175.00	
0041	Furniture/Fixture Depreciation		1,910.00
0050	Motor Vehicles	30,500.00	
0051	Motor Vehicles Depreciation		9,500.00
1001	Stock	12,000.00	
1100	Debtors Control Account	12,500.00	
1103	Prepayments	300.00	
1106	Provision for doubtful debts		1,250.00
1200	Bank Current Account	1,350.00	
2100	Creditors Control Account		6,575.00
2109	Accruals		300.00
2202	VAT Liability		2,500.00
3000	Keith Thompson Capital Account		10,000.00
3001	Annabel Harrison Capital Account		10,000.00
3002	Harley Clifford Capital Account		5,000.00
3060	Keith Thompson Current Account	1,250.00	
3061	Annabel Harrison Current Account		3,050.00
3062	Harley Clifford Capital Account		2,500.00
4000	Sales		220,000.00
4200	Sales of Assets	400.00	
5000	Purchases	150,000.00	
5200	Opening Stock	34,050.00	
5201	Closing Stock		12,000.00
6201	Advertising	1,350.00	
7003	Staff Salaries	22,000.00	
7100	Rent	1,200.00	
7103	General Rates	600.00	
7200	Electricity	450.00	
7304	Miscellaneous Motor Expenses	1,300.00	
7550	Telephone and Fax	650.00	
7800	Repairs and Renewals	350.00	
8000	Depreciation	8,165.00	
8102	Bad Debt Provision	775.00	
8204	Insurance	200.00	
8250	Sundry Expenses	250.00	
	Totals:	286,815.00	286,815.00

Date: 09/07/2013   **Hair Care Supplies Ltd**   Page: 1
Time: 12:45:15   **Balance Sheet**

From: Month 1, April 2012
To: Month 12, March 2013

Chart of Accounts: Default Layout of Accounts

	Period		Year to Date	
Fixed Assets				
Office Equipment	770.00		770.00	
Furniture and Fixtures	2,265.00		2,265.00	
Motor Vehicles	21,000.00		21,000.00	
		24,035.00		24,035.00
Current Assets				
Stock	12,000.00		12,000.00	
Debtors	11,550.00		11,550.00	
Bank Account	1,350.00		1,350.00	
		24,900.00		24,900.00
Current Liabilities				
Creditors : Short Term	6,875.00		6,875.00	
VAT Liability	2,500.00		2,500.00	
		9,375.00		9,375.00
Current Assets less Current Liabilities:		15,525.00		15,525.00
Total Assets less Current Liabilities:		39,560.00		39,560.00
Long Term Liabilities				
		0.00		0.00
Total Assets less Total Liabilities:		39,560.00		39,560.00
Capital & Reserves				
Capital	29,300.00		29,300.00	
P & L Account	10,260.00		10,260.00	
		39,560.00		39,560.00

Date: 09/07/2013	Hair Care Supplies Ltd	Page: 1
Time: 12:45:54	Profit and Loss	

From: Month 1, April 2012
To: Month 12, March 2013

Chart of Accounts: Default Layout of Accounts

	Period		Year to Date	
Sales				
Product Sales	220,000.00		220,000.00	
Sales of Assets	(400.00)		(400.00)	
		219,600.00		219,600.00
Purchases				
Purchases	150,000.00		150,000.00	
Stock	22,050.00		22,050.00	
		172,050.00		172,050.00
Direct Expenses				
Sales Promotion	1,350.00		1,350.00	
		1,350.00		1,350.00
Gross Profit/(Loss):		46,200.00		46,200.00
Overheads				
Gross Wages	22,000.00		22,000.00	
Rent and Rates	1,800.00		1,800.00	
Heat, Light and Power	450.00		450.00	
Motor Expenses	1,300.00		1,300.00	
Telephone and Computer charges	650.00		650.00	
Maintenance	350.00		350.00	
Depreciation	8,165.00		8,165.00	
Bad Debts	775.00		775.00	
General Expenses	450.00		450.00	
		35,940.00		35,940.00
Net Profit/(Loss):		10,260.00		10,260.00

Task 3

When you process the year end on SAGE, you will see the following report:

No	Item	Type	A/C	Date	Ref	Details	Net	Tax	Gross
						Date: 09/07/2013 **Hair Care Supplies Ltd** **Page:** 1			
						Time: 12:51:31 **Year End Report**			
87	1	JD	4000	31/03/2013	Ledger	Ledger Year End	220,000.00	0.00	220,000.00
88	1	JC	4200	31/03/2013	Ledger	Ledger Year End	400.00	0.00	400.00
89	1	JC	5000	31/03/2013	Ledger	Ledger Year End	150,000.00	0.00	150,000.00
90	1	JC	5200	31/03/2013	Ledger	Ledger Year End	34,050.00	0.00	34,050.00
91	1	JD	5201	31/03/2013	Ledger	Ledger Year End	12,000.00	0.00	12,000.00
92	1	JC	6201	31/03/2013	Ledger	Ledger Year End	1,350.00	0.00	1,350.00
93	1	JC	7003	31/03/2013	Ledger	Ledger Year End	22,000.00	0.00	22,000.00
94	1	JC	7100	31/03/2013	Ledger	Ledger Year End	1,200.00	0.00	1,200.00
95	1	JC	7103	31/03/2013	Ledger	Ledger Year End	600.00	0.00	600.00
96	1	JC	7200	31/03/2013	Ledger	Ledger Year End	450.00	0.00	450.00
97	1	JC	7304	31/03/2013	Ledger	Ledger Year End	1,300.00	0.00	1,300.00
98	1	JC	7550	31/03/2013	Ledger	Ledger Year End	650.00	0.00	650.00
99	1	JC	7800	31/03/2013	Ledger	Ledger Year End	350.00	0.00	350.00
100	1	JC	8000	31/03/2013	Ledger	Ledger Year End	8,165.00	0.00	8,165.00
101	1	JC	8102	31/03/2013	Ledger	Ledger Year End	775.00	0.00	775.00
102	1	JC	8204	31/03/2013	Ledger	Ledger Year End	200.00	0.00	200.00
103	1	JC	8250	31/03/2013	Ledger	Ledger Year End	250.00	0.00	250.00
104	1	JC	3200	31/03/2013	Ledger	Ledger Year End	10,260.00	0.00	10,260.00

Here, you can see that there is a total profit for the year of £10,260 which needs to be allocated amongst the partners.

Remember that any salaries and interest will need to be dealt with before allocating the remaining profit.

Annabel will be paid a salary of £4,000 p.a. from 1 November 2012 onwards. Therefore, she is due a salary of £4,000 × 5/12 = £1,667.

This should be entered on SAGE using the journal below:

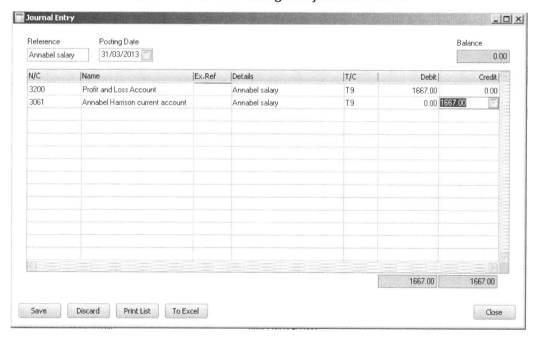

The remaining profit to be allocated between the partners is the balance of £8,593 shown on N/C3200 Profit and Loss Account on SAGE

You will need to allocate this profit amongst the three partners, using the profit-sharing ratio of 2:2:1

These will be allocated to the partners' current accounts as follows:

Keith: £3,437

Annabel: £3,437

Harley: £1,719

Your journal should agree to the one shown below:

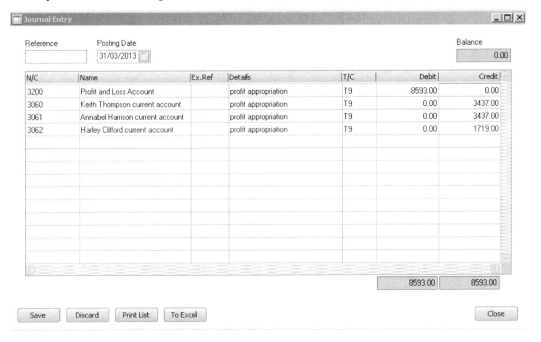

Task 4

Your opening Balance Sheet and opening Trial Balance at 1 April 2013 should be the same as the ones shown below:

Date: 23/05/2014	**Hair Care Supplies**	Page: 1
Time: 12:56:13	**Balance Sheet**	

From: Month 1, April 2013
To: Month 12, March 2014

Chart of Accounts: Default Layout of Accounts

	Period		Year to Date
Fixed Assets			
Office Equipment	0.00		770.00
Furniture and Fixtures	0.00		2,265.00
Motor Vehicles	0.00		21,000.00
		0.00	24,035.00
Current Assets			
Stock	0.00		12,000.00
Debtors	0.00		11,550.00
Bank Account	0.00		1,350.00
		0.00	24,900.00
Current Liabilities			
Creditors : Short Term	0.00		6,875.00
VAT Liability	0.00		2,500.00
		0.00	9,375.00
Current Assets less Current Liabilities:		0.00	15,525.00
Total Assets less Current Liabilities:		0.00	39,560.00
Long Term Liabilities			
		0.00	0.00
Total Assets less Total Liabilities:		0.00	39,560.00
Capital & Reserves			
Capital	0.00		39,560.00
P & L Account	0.00		0.00
		0.00	39,560.00

Date: 23/05/2014   **Hair Care Supplies**   **Page:** 1
Time: 12:56:53   **Period Trial Balance**

To Period: Month 12, March 2014

N/C	Name	Debit	Credit
0030	Computer Equipment	3,000.00	
0031	Computer Equipment Depreciation		2,230.00
0040	Furniture and Fixtures	4,175.00	
0041	Furniture/Fixture Depreciation		1,910.00
0050	Motor Vehicles	30,500.00	
0051	Motor Vehicles Depreciation		9,500.00
1001	Stock	12,000.00	
1100	Debtors Control Account	12,500.00	
1103	Prepayments	300.00	
1106	Provision for doubtful debts		1,250.00
1200	Bank Current Account	1,350.00	
2100	Creditors Control Account		6,575.00
2109	Accruals		300.00
2202	VAT Liability		2,500.00
3000	Keith Thompson capital account		10,000.00
3001	Annabel Harrison capital account		10,000.00
3002	Harley Clifford capital account		5,000.00
3060	Keith Thompson current account		2,187.00
3061	Annabel Harrison current account		8,154.00
3062	Harley Clifford current account		4,219.00
	Totals:	63,825.00	63,825.00

INDEX

Index